DATE DUE

Kingdom of Bahrain
The Financial Capital of the Middle East

Kingdom of Bahrain
The Financial Capital of the Middle East

by Philip Dew

Published by Euromoney Books

in association with

The Bahrain Monetary Agency

Published by
Euromoney Books
Nestor House
Playhouse Yard
London EC4V 5EX
Tel: +44 (0) 20 7779 8999 or USA +1 800 437 9997
Fax: +44 (0) 20 7779 8300
www.euromoneybooks.com
E-mail:hotline@euromoneyplc.com

ISBN 1 85564 982 9

Typeset by Julie Foster
Printed in Dubai by Emirates Printing Press

Contents

Contents

Acknowledgements

Philip Dew has lived and worked in the Arab World for approaching 35 years, a considerable proportion of which has been in Bahrain (16 years) and Saudi Arabia (12 years). After employment in the banking sector in the United Kingdom and the Middle East he established his own business development consultancy in 1982. This has focused largely on industrial and business development in the Gulf Cooperation Council States, especially in Bahrain and Saudi Arabia, but assignments in Egypt, Jordan, Yemen, Iran, Iraq, Cyprus, Greece, Lebanon and Syria have also been concluded. Integral to Philip Dew's activities over the past twenty years has been participation in a number of conferences, seminars, symposia and workshops on economic development in the Gulf States and as consultant editor of a number of practical guides on doing business in the region including titles on Yemen, the UAE, Bahrain, Iran, Oman, Qatar and Cyprus. He is also author of *Saudi Arabia: Restructuring for Growth*, a Euromoney publication published in January 2003.

Philip Dew would like to thank all of the following people in the Bahrain Monetary Agency for their kind help in researching this book:

H.E. The Governor, Shaikh Ahmed bin Mohammed Al Khalifa; H.E. The Deputy Governor, Khalid Abdulla Al Bassam; Dr. Naser M.Y.Al Belooshi, Executive Director – Corporate Services; Dr. Khalid Abdulla Ateeq, Executive Director – Banking Supervision; Anwar Khalifa Al-Sadah, Executive Director – Financial Institutions

Supervision; Waleed Abdulla Rashdan, Executive Director, Banking Operations; Ahmed Isa Al Somaim, Director, Reserve Management Directorate; Dr. Abdul Rahman Ali Saif, Director, Economic Research Directorate; Yousef Rashid Al Fadhel, Director, Information Technology Directorate; Ali Salman Thamer, Director Capital Markets Supervision Directorate; Shaikh Salman bin Isa Al Khalifa, Director, Islamic Financial Institutions Directorate; Tawfiq Isa Shehab, Director, Insurance Supervision Directorate; Abdul Rahman Mohammed Al-Baker, Director, Financial Institutions Supervision Directorate; Shaikha Hessa bint Ali Al Khalifa, Head of Licensing and Information Unit; Abbas M. Radhi, Director of Currency Issue; Khalid Hamad A. Rahman, Director of Banking Supervision Directorate; Yousuf Mohammed Bahar, Head – Money Market; Ahmed Jassim Bumtaia, Head of Economic Research; Abdulla Khamis Al-Sulaiti, Head – Currency Issue; Farid Jassim Zubari, Head of Banking Services Directorate; Yousif Ahmed Al-Tamimi, Local Financial Market Superintendent, Banking Services Directorate; Saleh Isa AlMehri, Superintendent Islamic Banks, Islamic Financial Institutions Directorate; Abdul Ameer Thamer, Financial Analyst, Financial Institutions Supervision Directorate; John Field, Brian Kettell, Ralph Ricks and Ashley Freeman, Advisors; Rima Al-Kilani and Farah Mattar, Promotion and Media Unit; Nader Yousuf Ahmed Rashdan, The Deputy Governor's Office; Anita Al-Hussaini.

Thanks are due also to the following people in other institutions who gave freely of their time to assist in providing information for the book:

Murad Ali Murad, Chairman, Bank of Bahrain and Kuwait; Saleh S. AlKowari, Chief Executive Officer, HSBC Bank Middle East; Atif A. Abdulmalik, Chief Executive Officer, First Islamic Investment Bank; Adnan Ahmed Yousef, Chief Executive Officer, Bahrain Islamic Bank; Jean-Christophe Durand, Regional Director-GCC Countries, BNP Paribas; Adnan Sharabi, Regional Manager, The Housing Bank for Trade and Finance – Jordan; Claus Buchi, Executive Director, UBS AG; Nazem Ibrahim-Basha, Director, Global Private Clients and Jonathan Crosse, Vice President, Senior Financial Advisor, Merrill Lynch International Bank Limited; Hani Fadayel, Senior Vice President and Senior Manager, Arab Bank plc; Paul Bradford, Vice President, International Division, Arab Banking Corporation; Ali Ahmed Al-Mansoor, Head of Public Relations, Bahrain Stock Exchange; Khalid A. AlHajeri, Senior Public Relations Specialist, Bahrain Stock Exchange; Abdul Rais Abdul Majid, Chief Executive Officer,

International Islamic Financial Market; Sameer Al-Wazzan, Chairman, Bahrain Insurance Association; Iain Reid, Regional Director, Norwich Union Middle East and Bahrain Insurance Association Director, Property, Casualty and Marine; Michael Davey, The Housing Bank; Hussain Ismail, Deputy Director, Bahrain Institute of Banking and Finance; Wendy Toorani, Executive Manager, Bankers' Society of Bahrain; Christopher Fairey, De La Rue Currency; Kevin Moriarty; Glyn Davies, Manager Treasury and Fixed Income, BNP Paribas; Jeremy Jaquet, Bank of Bahrain and Kuwait; Meir Nonoo, Managing Director, Bahrain Financing Company.

Preface

Bahrain has been at the heart of international trade for many millennia, first as an entrepot between Mesopotamia and the Indus Valley and then as a focal point for the sale of pearls in exchange for goods with merchants across the Indian Ocean. Today, however, Bahrain is best known as the leading international financial centre in the Middle East.

Banking first came to Bahrain in 1921 and remained modest in scale for the succeeding 50 years. Then, in the early 1970s, increased wealth across the Middle East created the demand for a high level of banking and financial services, which Bahrain was well-placed to provide. Concurrent with this was the formation of the Bahrain Monetary Agency (BMA), which was to play such an important role in developing Bahrain into the global financial market it is today, with almost 350 banks, financial institutions and insurance and capital market companies from across the globe maintaining presences.

The growth of Bahrain into a financial centre of international stature has taken little more than a quarter of a century and could not have been achieved without the perception and foresight of the country's rulers, who have ensured political and economic stability, or those closely involved with the BMA, who have pursued the attainment and maintenance of a regulatory and supervisory regime dedicated to the application of the most stringent global standards.

As the Kingdom of Bahrain moves forward into a new era, with the BMA as the country's single regulatory authority for the financial sector, the publication of this book is timely. It places the international financial centre in historical context by looking back to the early decades of the 20th century, when the first bank in the region opened its doors, through to the present day, highlighting the landmarks along the way.

In covering these 80 years, attention has been given to the growth of banking and finance in the country, including detailed information on every licensed sector; the birth and rise in importance of the Bahrain Currency Board and its successor the BMA; and the development of the overall banking and financial sector's regulatory environment. The book also examines the growth of the insurance sector from humble beginnings in the early 1950s; the birth and rise of the Bahrain Stock Exchange; the ongoing relationships of the BMA with international bodies such as the International Monetary Fund, the Basel Committee and the Financial Action Task Force; and the vital importance of education and training to the overall growth of the sector.

In conclusion, the book considers the future of banking and finance in Bahrain and of the BMA as a unitary regulatory authority. In so doing, the book recognises that Bahrain, as the financial capital of the Middle East, must continue to develop and progress if it is to maintain its status amongst its peers worldwide, whilst also ensuring continued compliance with international norms of supervision and corporate governance. The evidence suggests Bahrain, the BMA and all those individuals most directly involved, be they in government or the private sector, are well placed to face this challenge.

1 Introduction

Bahrain as a centre of trade and commerce throughout history

Bahrain has been at the heart of trade and commerce in the Arabian Gulf for nearly 5,000 years, having once been an important entrepôt on the major trade routes, a role it continued to fulfil well into the second half of the twentieth century. Over the years, the country was also to become a leading player in the world pearling industry, then the first Gulf country to strike oil and, more recently, the well-established international financial centre of global repute it is today. Although throughout the centuries, Bahrain's location mid-way between west and east has helped it to ensure a prominent position, in more recent years it has been the education and skills of the Kingdom's people allied to the government's desire to diversify and grow the national economy that have had an increasingly important role to play.

Archaeologists sifting through the detritus of those five millennia have ascertained that Dilmun, as Bahrain was known as far back as 2,800 BC, was a major port and harbour on the important trading route between Mesopotamia, modern day Iraq, and the civilisations of the Indus valley, in today's Pakistan. There were two primary reasons for the country's status at that time: its location close to the eastern seaboard of Arabia, which allowed ships to sail in the lee of the coast through Bahrain to and from the northern Gulf safe from storms, and the ready availability of fresh water both onshore and offshore, which may well have given rise to the islands' Arabic name, which means two seas.

Given the country's strategic position, and the ready availability of fresh water, Bahrain has been, over time, coveted by successive powers intent on gaining control

Diplomatic area

over the Gulf region. Thus, over the centuries the Sumerians, the Greeks (following the discovery of the islands, which they knew as Tylos, by Alexander the Great), the Persians, the Portuguese, central Arabian tribes, Ottoman Turks and, in the more recent few hundred years, the British have all sought and attained control over the islands. Despite such undoubted interest by foreign powers, until the third decade of the twentieth century the people of Bahrain were able to do little more than eke out an existence from limited agricultural and fishing activities and, most importantly, from the revenues derived from pearl diving and the resulting trade, as vessels returned from faraway places, mainly the Indian sub-continent, carrying cargoes of gold, spices and other valuable commodities that their captains had exchanged for their prized pearls.

This international trade also provided many non-financial benefits to the people of Bahrain as it enabled them to hone their trading skills in what had become a highly cosmopolitan environment, whilst many of their near neighbours faced severe hardships. Such an international outlook, which included trade with all countries in the region as well as across the Indian Ocean, led to Bahrain becoming the first Gulf country to establish schools, other than Islamic *madrasahs,* such that by the time the pearling industry faced its ultimate decline late in the 1920s, due in large part to the introduction of the cultured pearl, and the finding of oil early in the next decade, many of the population, both male and female, were already well-educated.

Although oil had been found many years earlier in Iran and Iraq, Bahrain became the first state in the Gulf, in 1932, to find and exploit it commercially. Having found the famous black gold Bahrain became something of an El Dorado among the peoples of the Gulf littoral, who sought energetically to work in the country, although in the event Bahrain's resources were to prove meagre by comparison with those of its neighbours. Following on from this initial success, crude oil was first exported in 1934 and Bahrain's refinery, which remains in production today, commenced production in 1936.

The economy diversifies and the financial sector grows more important

As time passed, Bahrain's successive rulers intuitively recognised the limitations imposed by dependence on a single natural resource, especially one whose price could and did fluctuate considerably according to world demand, and so sought ways and means of diversifying the economy. Thus, in the 1960s, recognising that in addition to oil the country had a not inconsiderable supply of natural gas, the government sought to develop industry, a development which has proven most successful. Subsequently, in the 1970s, a move was made into the banking and finance sector and, in more recent years, into tourism. In support of this diversification a strong infrastructure was put in place allied to which were a broad range of incentives to encourage foreign companies to come to Bahrain, including the creation of liberal investment and ownership laws and the absence of either corporate or personal taxation. These moves have proved most beneficial although oil continues to be a major revenue earner for the government and, indeed, is in many years the prime source of income.

Since independence in 1971, Bahrain's programme of diversification has been an undoubted success with the banking and financial sector a major factor. Since the formation of the BMA in 1973 the financial sector has grown to such an extent that as at mid-2003 there were almost 350 banking and financial institutions, including insurance and insurance-related companies, based in the Kingdom, many of them foreign owned.

This large number of international entities contributes directly to the country's revenues in the form of fees and in economic value through expenditure on goods and services and the employment and development of the nation's human resources. These banking and financial communities also contribute indirectly to the national economy in terms of expansion of both trade and services, especially in the form of tourism, real estate, transportation, telecommunications and the creation of job opportunities outside the financial sector.

A major element in the growth of Bahrain as the financial capital of the Middle East has been the provision of employment in the sector for the country's well-educated workforce. Through the development of the international financial centre and the provision of excellent training and education in banking and financial matters, the financial sector can today boast a high level of Bahrainisation – nearly 90 per cent of all employees, both male and female, in full commercial banks and in excess of 75 per cent of all employees in international banks.

In terms of GDP, the banking, finance and insurance sector has grown to become a major contributor, having at one time been no more than a minor element in the figures. In 1970 banking and insurance contributed just BD1.3 million (US$3.3 million) to the total GDP of BD116.3 million (US$308 million), or 1.1 per cent, figures which had increased to BD93.2 million (US$247 million) or 10.11 per cent of the total of BD921.8 million (US$2.4 billion) by 1981 – the first year banking and finance attained a double figure share of the total.

In subsequent years, with a brief exception in the late 1980s and early 1990s, when the sector was affected by regional instability, the financial sector has continued to increase its share of GDP, such that by 1997, and for the succeeding two years, it had become the major contributor to GDP with a share in excess of 21 per cent and a value which had reached BD537.17 million (US$1.4 billion) in 1999. In 2000 and

Artist's impression of future Bahrain Financial Harbour project

2001 world oil prices rose again and the Kingdom's oil and gas sector regained its status as the major contributor to GDP although in 2000 the banking and finance sector made its highest-ever contribution in value terms at BD640.01 million (US$1.7 billion). Throughout the growth of the sector, the international banking community has been a major contributor to the financial sector's share in total GDP, as the figures in Exhibit 1.1 show. As can be seen, the offshore banks' contribution to the overall financial sector has varied between 48.4 per cent and 53.9 per cent throughout the defined period.

Exhibit 1.1: GDP at current prices, 1997-2001 (BD million)

Sector	*1997*	*1998*	*1999*	*2000*	*2001*
Oil and gas	441.70	311.39	448.07	835.68	731.79
Financial corporations	504.53	532.86	537.17	640.01	557.93
- onshore banks	126.82	140.28	138.58	167.56	165.15
- offshore banks	244.37	265.74	289.62	344.56	296.44
- insurance	133.34	126.84	108.98	127.89	96.35
Other	1,441.08	1,480.96	1,504.03	1,521.24	1,693.77
Total GDP					
(at purchasers' prices)	**2,387.31**	**2,325.21**	**2,489.27**	**2,996.93**	**2,983.49**

Source: National Accounts 2001, Directorate of Economic Planning, Ministry of Finance and National Economy.

The status of Bahrain as the financial capital of the Middle East

Bahrain's status as a major financial centre has in large part been brought about by the political, social and economic stability which prevails in the country. Integral to this has been the government's desire over many years to pursue a prudent fiscal policy, to ensure on-going diversification of the country's economic activities and to attain and maintain monetary stability.

This approach has clearly paid dividends as three international ratings agencies have seen fit in the recent past to raise their ratings for Bahrain. The first to do so was Fitch Ratings when it upgraded Bahrain's long-term foreign currency rating to A- (from BBB), its short-term local currency rating to F1 (from F3) and the long-term local currency rating to A (from BBB). Subsequently, Standard & Poor's raised its long-term foreign currency sovereign credit rating to A- and its long-term local currency rating to A and then, a month later, Moody's Investors Service raised the foreign currency ceiling on Bahrain's bonds to investment grade Baa3 from an earlier speculative Ba1. Most importantly, the agencies perceived the future risk outlook for Bahrain to be stable.

Such improvements in Bahrain's ratings express confidence in the progress being made in the country thereby strengthening the status of its economy in financial and economic circles worldwide. They ensure also the most favourable conditions for attracting foreign investment thereby enhancing the leading role of Bahrain as a destination of choice for international financial institutions seeking a presence in the region.

These on-going positive developments have been wholly integral to Bahrain's position today as the financial centre of the Middle East. In the 1960s, before its descent into civil war and chaos, Lebanon undoubtedly had the prime role as a banking centre for the region. But that was forfeited during the long years of civil strife in the 1970s and 1980s and, although the rebuilding of Lebanon may see it re-emerge as an important financial centre in the future, Bahrain has made great leaps forward in the interim. It is unique in offering complex financial services in a time zone located conveniently between Asia and Europe and with a depth and capacity to service the needs of clients throughout the Middle East, as well as those further afield. Within the Gulf, there are other states with ambitions to develop financial services centres for the region, but these are relatively late entrants in comparison with Bahrain and lack the long track record and the tradition of sound regulation that international investors seek for reassurance.

It is the depth and breadth of Bahrain's long-established financial services sector that give substance to its position as an important global financial market. Bahrain has addressed the issues surrounding the availability of adequate numbers of skilled, affordable workers by investing in the training and education of the indigenous workforce. The breadth of Bahrain's financial services sector is apparent from the number of banking institutions established in the country, both conventional and Islamic, as well as the growth in the number of services offered, including a broad range of Islamic banking services, as well as insurance, trusts and collective investment schemes.

The authorities – principally the Bahrain Monetary Agency (BMA) – have adopted a realistic regulatory and policy framework within which to allow financial services to flourish. An absence of foreign exchange controls and a policy of pegging the Bahraini dinar to the US dollar have provided a mixture of flexibility and stability that facilitates international financial flows. At the same time, the BMA has taken steps to ensure that Bahrain complies with important international initiatives that protect the integrity of the financial centre. It has supported the anti-money laundering initiatives of the Financial Action Task Force on Money Laundering (FATF), and its Central Risk Unit plays an important part in overseeing lending by commercial banks to reduce credit risks. It has also taken on an important role in consumer protection – not always a central bank responsibility – to ensure that compliance with international initiatives is not compromised by a neglect of the day-to-day concerns facing both the retail and corporate users of financial services in Bahrain. A liberal yet well-defined policy framework has encouraged more international institutions to establish a presence in the Kingdom and this has created a virtuous circle whereby these institutions help to ensure that the latest techniques are employed in the Bahraini financial services sector.

Bahrain has also been determined to maintain its competitive edge *vis à vis* other financial centres and to continue adding to the range of services on offer. The recent moves to encourage the establishment of trusts, for instance, mark a challenge to the more established financial centres, which have a longer record in servicing this part of the offshore industry. In the area of collective investment schemes, too, the BMA has crafted a legal and fiscal regime that is intended to give Bahrain's offerings an edge over existing centres. Insurance legislation is also being upgraded in response to the growing complexity of the sector and in order to make Bahrain a more competitive centre internationally. But it is in the area of Islamic finance that it has most clearly established a comparative advantage over any competitors. It has worked closely with the Islamic Development Bank (IDB) in establishing the Islamic financial centre in Bahrain and has been rewarded with the largest concentration of Islamic financial institutions in the Middle East. This numerical presence has been complemented by a growth in the range of products being offered through Islamic financial institutions in Bahrain, including leasing, syndicated lending and collective investment schemes. In addition, several support organisations have been set up in Bahrain: the Accounting and Auditing Organization for Islamic Financial Institutions (AAOIFI); the International Islamic Rating Agency (IIRA); the Liquidity Management Centre (LMC); the Islamic Financial Services Board (IFSB); General Council for Islamic Banks and Financial Institutions (GCIBFI); and the International Islamic Financial Market (IIFM).

New initiatives

Many new initiatives have been introduced by the BMA since 2002 to further advance the banking and finance industry in Bahrain, so as to maintain its position as the leading international financial centre in the Middle East. An important step in this regard was the recent move to make the BMA the sole regulator for the entire financial services industry, comprising not only banks and financial institutions but also investment firms, insurance companies, the Bahrain Stock Exchange and all other specialised financial services providers. Furthermore, the BMA is also implementing a multifaceted strategy aimed at introducing and developing several asset classes deemed to have high growth potential. Integral to these are corporate and private banking, debt and equity capital markets, insurance and reinsurance, remote services and leasing, all of which will, wherever possible, address both conventional and Islamic requirements.

A major new private sector initiative is the Bahrain Financial Harbour, which is to be developed on Manama sea front. This one billion dollar project will create an integrated, state-of-the-art environment for the financial industry in Bahrain supported by world class telecommunications and information technology platforms conducive to encouraging an increasing number of global financial institutions to the country.

Over the years, the Kingdom's success as an international financial centre has been built on the breadth and depth of markets opened up for investment and the products and services they offer, fully supported by a policy of rigorous regulation and supervision to the highest international standards. With a confirmed policy of continuous enhancement of the regulatory environment and the ongoing introduction of advanced financial products and services Bahrain, the financial capital of the Middle East, seems set for continued progress.

2
The banking industry in Bahrain

The origins of the banking industry

Given Bahrain's role as an important centre of trade, with the country's harbour once named 'the port of the Arabian Gulf', it is unsurprising to learn that the major business of the early banks was trade finance as well as the taking of deposits.

From modest beginnings in 1921 the small banking community witnessed a major transition of the economy over the following 70 years. With the discovery of oil on the islands in 1932, the economy no longer depended totally on pearl diving, agriculture and trade. The consequent development of Bahrain as a location for major industrial projects was followed by the strategic decision in the 1970s to develop the financial services sector as a pivotal component of diversification away from natural resources and which led to the importance of Bahrain as an international financial hub – a transition few could have imagined all those years earlier.

The first banks

It was in 1921 when the Eastern Bank first opened its doors. Following a takeover in 1957 its name changed to the Chartered Bank, which today has become the Standard Chartered Bank.

The banking services offered were rudimentary with transactions recorded by hand. The Eastern Bank branch was located on part of the upper floor of a house rented from a prominent pearl merchant, where the branch manager also maintained his residence and below which goods were stored.

British Bank of the Middle East, Manama, 1940s

Eastern Bank, Muharraq Branch, 1950s

Nevertheless, the services provided were adequate to the demands of the populace and the business community. It was not until 24 years later that another bank, the Imperial Bank of Iran, established a presence in Bahrain. It later became The British Bank of the Middle East (in 1952, having briefly been The British Bank of Iran and the Middle East) and ultimately HSBC Middle East.

Arab Bank, Manama, 1960

Chartered Bank, Main Branch, Manama, 1965

The first largely locally owned institution was set up 13 years later, the Bank of Bahrain, whose successor is now the Kingdom's largest domestic bank, National Bank of Bahrain. The Arab Bank of Jordan became the fourth bank in 1960.

The formation of the Bank of Bahrain in 1956 was a watershed in Bahrain's banking history as it brought together a number of local businessmen as major shareholders of a banking entity for the first time. Following issuance of Amiri Decree No.31 of 1956 the Bank was established with an authorised capital of Indian rupees 10 million (equivalent to approximately BD1 million), 50 per cent paid-up; of which 75 per cent was owned by the Bahraini founders, who included a number of senior representatives of prominent local business families. The 25 per cent share was originally held by a number of foreign institutions and individuals but later became fully owned by National and Grindlays Bank Limited, which also provided the management of the bank in its early years.

The bank commenced operations from a modest apartment overlooking Al Khalifa Avenue on 2 January 1957, restricting its activities in what has been described as: 'the true tradition of a local bank', to domestic retail and commercial banking.

In early 1973 the government of Bahrain obtained approval from the bank's Board of Directors to purchase the 25 per cent owned by National and Grindlays Bank and over the ensuing months increased its holding to 49 per cent of the Bank's capital by acquiring 25,000 new shares. It was at this time the bank became known as the National Bank of Bahrain with its capital doubled to BD2 million as a result of the government's purchase.

Self-regulating banks

Throughout this period of change, Bahrain's banks were largely self-regulating. In fact, the IMF remarked in September 1972 that there were: 'no regulations covering banking activities at this time'. However, the foreign banks were undoubtedly guided by their Head Offices and, in part at least, by the Bank of England, as Bahrain was for many years a full member of the Sterling Area. A major impact of this latter involvement was that all foreign exchange surpluses were invested in the United Kingdom in Treasury Bills or government securities, as was required under the then current regulations.

Monetary reform: the Bahrain Currency Board

Replacement of the Indian rupee with the Gulf rupee

Up until the beginning of the nineteenth century financial and commercial dealings had been carried out through commonly circulated currencies such as the Austrian taler, the Turkish lira and the Indian rupee. However, the increase in the rate of trade between Bahrain and India, especially the pearl trade, made the Indian rupee the most commonly circulated currency in Bahrain. Therefore, the Indian rupee was promoted from a currency that could only be circulated or exchanged in 1818, into the official currency of the country in 1880. The Indian rupee maintained its role as the official currency of the islands until it had become subject to large-scale smuggling, partly in exchange for foreign currencies but more importantly, as a medium of exchange for unofficial gold bullion shipments being imported into India.

In 1959, the Indian Government introduced the Gulf rupee with a value equivalent to the currency it was replacing. Whilst the new currency was introduced mainly to assist the Government of India to overcome a situation which may otherwise have led to devaluation of its currency and severe damage to its emerging domestic economy, it was intended also as an interim measure between the usage of the Indian currency and the issuance by the Arabian Gulf States of their own currencies.

In 1961 HH Shaikh Isa bin Salman Al Khalifa, the father of the present King, HM Shaikh Hamad bin Isa Al Khalifa, became Ruler. High on his personal agenda was monetary reform and in 1964, Amiri Decree No. 6 Finance was promulgated declaring that the Gulf rupee was to be superceded by a national currency to be known as the Bahraini dinar.

The country's new national currency was first issued in October 1965 and in the same year, a further Amiri Decree, No. 7 Finance, declared the formation of the Bahrain Currency Board. The foundation of the Currency Board was really a turning point in the history of Bahrain's economy as the board issued successive decisions that sought to regularise the monetary situation in the country. This monetary authority was also charged with issuing and circulating the new currency and, subsequently, with being the authority responsible for the granting of banking licences.

The launch of the Bahraini dinar

The Bahraini dinar was from the outset freely convertible. Divided into 1,000 fils, it was fully backed by gold and foreign exchange for which a currency reserve fund was established, although the Currency Board would only redeem the new notes for foreign currency – not for gold. Nevertheless the Board's decision to make the currency freely exchangeable, and in ensuring its ease of conversion from the Gulf rupee, ensured its rapid acceptance.

Changeover from Indian rupees to Bahrain dinars at Chartered Bank, October 1965

In October 1965, the first coins and banknotes were issued in 11 denominations – six coins (100 fils, 50 fils, 25 fils, ten fils, five fils and one fils) and five banknotes (10 dinars, 5 dinars, one dinar, half a dinar and a quarter dinar). Subsequently, in 1968, a further banknote was also introduced with the denomination of 100 fils. The denominations selected for the new currency were particularly important during the transition period as they made the conversion from Gulf rupees very easy as 100 fils was valued at one rupee; 50 fils equated to 50 paisa; the quarter dinar was worth 2.5 rupees; the one dinar, 10 rupees; and the five and 10 dinars 50 and 100 rupees respectively. This first issue of Bahraini dinars also circulated in the Emirate of Abu Dhabi between 1965 and 1971, when it was replaced there by the UAE Dirham, following the formation of the United Arab Emirates.

At the outset the new currency had its value fixed at 1.86621 grams of pure gold and, to ensure a smooth transition from the rupee, sterling was used as an intervention currency, with the new Bahraini dinar being valued at 15 English shillings, which at the time was equal to 10 Indian or Gulf rupees. The change from the Gulf rupee to the dinar was subject also to a redemption agreement with the Reserve Bank of India under which payments were to be made in sterling over a period of 10 years. Stability of the sterling/dinar exchange rate in these early years was vital to the day-to-day management of the new currency and as a result the daily exchange rates quoted by the Currency Board remained unchanged until 18 November 1967, when sterling was devalued by 14.3 per cent.

Since the gold parity of the dinar remained unchanged, this devaluation had a markedly adverse impact on the Currency Board as heavy book losses were occasioned which, in the event, were made good by the Government of Bahrain. The banks operating locally at the time also faced similar losses. As a result of this event, and as part of the national exchange rate policy, the buying and selling rates of the dinar began to be linked to the US dollar as well as to sterling. Such a move gave protection to the dinar and helped contain exchange rate fluctuations to a minimum.

This devaluation was to be the first of a number of uncertainties in the local currency markets, including devaluations of the dollar in 1971 and again in 1973, following cessation of its linkage to gold, and concurrent worldwide monetary instability. Despite these problems the overall stability of the dinar was maintained but over time the currency became formally pegged to the SDR with the dollar remaining as the intervention currency.

The background to the foundation of the Bahrain Monetary Agency (BMA)

It was at the time of all this volatility in the foreign exchange markets of the early 1970s that the decision was taken to replace the Bahrain Currency Board with the BMA which, in the event, was to have much wider responsibilities than its predecessor.

The proliferation of banks in Bahrain and the need for more control

Until 1960 Bahrain had been well served by just three banks, but between that year and 1971 a further eight banks were granted banking licences by the Bahrain Currency Board to operate in the country, bringing the total to eleven commercial banks by the end of the latter year.

Growth in the domestic economy

During the late 1960s, the ruler, HH Shaikh Isa bin Salman Al Khalifa, had recognised the finite nature of oil revenues and thus initiated a policy of economic diversification. Bahrain had identified an important source of natural gas within its borders and so, over the ensuing years, major gas-based industrial investments were implemented, the

Exhibit 2.1: Licensed commercial banks - to 1971

Name	*Year licensed*
Standard Chartered Bank	
(as Eastern Bank, initially authorised in 1918)	1920
HSBC Middle East	
(initially as The British Bank of Iran and the Middle East)	1944
National Bank of Bahrain	
(initially as Bank of Bahrain)	1957
Arab Bank	1960
Habib Bank Ltd.	1968
United Bank Ltd.	1969
Rafidain Bank	1969
Citibank N.A.	1969
Bank Melli Iran	1970
Chase Manhattan Bank	
(no longer maintains a commercial banking presence)	1971
Bank of Bahrain & Kuwait	1971

Source: Bahrain Monetary Agency, Licensing & Policy Directorate.

first being Aluminium Bahrain, which is, in 2003, among the world's largest aluminium smelters and still growing.

The rapid growth in the number of banks requesting licences to operate in Bahrain arose largely from the enhanced prosperity of the country and its neighbours, resulting from the increased returns being derived from oil. However, it was to be 1973 before the substantial rise in world oil prices led to yet greater wealth of the Gulf States. Further attractions for both the foreign banking community, and for local businessmen seeking to participate in the domestic banking sector, were the country's strong trading position; the relative proximity of Bahrain within the Arabian Gulf to more populous neighbours with less developed banking capabilities; the presence of large numbers of expatriates in Bahrain and elsewhere in the region requiring banking links with their homelands; the fact that Bahrainis were among the best educated populations of the Gulf states, education having been available for boys since 1919 and for girls since 1928; and, probably most importantly, the progressive approach taken towards economic development.

Although the number of commercial banks more than doubled between 1968 and 1971, the assets of the banks saw only modest growth. In 1968, the five banks then licensed had total assets of BD55.07 million (US$147.2 million), a figure which had risen to just BD99.49 million (US$266 million) four years later when there were 11 banks in operation – an overall increase of just 81 per cent over the four years, an average annual increase of 20.25 per cent. (Detailed figures appear in Chapter 4, Domestic banking.)

Increased competition and the need for regulation

Concurrent with this growth in the domestic economy were the demands of the business community and an increasing public awareness and acceptance of banks, and therefore their use. Thus those banks which had given longevity of service to Bahrain now found themselves having to meet the higher level of competition from the new arrivals in the sector. As a result, they moved away from their earlier base of trade finance and deposit-taking to offer the increasingly sophisticated and complex services the new arrivals were seeking to provide. Thus the nature of banking in Bahrain was enhanced and the need for greater regulation and supervision than had been available up to that time became necessary. This situation resulted, in 1971, in the decision being taken to move toward the formation of what became the BMA.

BMA: initial objectives and responsibilities

In 1971, following the full independence of Bahrain from Great Britain, one of the first steps taken by the government was the formation of a stronger monetary authority. Just two years later, under the terms of Amiri Decree No. 23 of 1973, the BMA came into being as an independent juristic body with clearly defined but sufficiently broadly based powers enabling fulfilment of the activities of a central monetary institution for the then State of Bahrain.

The initial objectives of this new entity were defined as the:

a. organisation of the issue and circulation of the currency of the State of Bahrain and the orderly functioning of local foreign exchange operations;
b. maintenance of the value of the currency of Bahrain and monetary stability;

c. organisation of the banking business and control of the banking system;
d. control and direction of bank credit so as to realise the objectives of the economic policy of the state;
e. participation in the creation of a developed money and financial market; and
f. role of fiscal agent of the government.

Integral to these objectives, the BMA was to be responsible for issuing all local currency; for maintaining its external value; for establishing and maintaining a foreign reserve providing not less than 100 per cent cover for the dinar, except in exceptional circumstances; and for establishing foreign exchange operations in the country. The first issue of currency, which has become known as The Bahrain Currency Board Issue, was superceded in 1979 by the so-called First Currency Issue introduced by the then

Gulf International Bank

six year old BMA, but nevertheless remained in circulation until finally being withdrawn in 1984.

Under the terms of the law, the BMA was vested with wide discretionary powers in establishing strong relations with both the government and the banking sector. In its governmental role the BMA was to become the government's banker and the depository of its funds, holding them either in-house or with a locally registered commercial bank on terms agreed with the Ministry of Finance, which has historically been the case, with the National Bank of Bahrain as the beneficiary depository. It was also to act as the government's fiscal agent and to be responsible for administering the National Debt; for advising the government on matters impacting on monetary stability, including recommendations as to remedial measures to be taken to ensure such stability; for investing and managing the country's foreign exchange reserves; for advancing short-term loans to cover any deficit arising in the National Budget; and for acting as financial agent through which all operations are transacted with international financial bodies of which Bahrain is a member.

The BMA's relations with banks and financial institutions were to be much the same as that between any central monetary authority and its local financial community. Thus the BMA, which seeks to exercise its role with all due discretion, is responsible for ensuring the smooth flow of transactions with banks by opening and maintaining accounts on their behalf, buying and selling a wide range of bills of exchange, government treasury notes and other like assets; for granting loans against securities; for ensuring banks maintain their reserve requirements; for specifying, according to the requirements of the government, the purposes for and terms on which credit may be granted; for setting and supervising controls on banking activities to ensure stability of and confidence in the overall banking sector; for establishing a clearing house; and for participation in any plan for insuring deposits which has been approved by the Minister of Finance.

Furthermore, the BMA was to be responsible for the issuance of licences for all banking and related financial institutions, except companies in the insurance sector and stock brokers, which were regulated at the time by the then Ministry of Commerce and Agriculture, and for rescinding them in case of need; for defining the nature of the business that banks and financial institutions may conduct; for establishing the level of capital and reserves and for stipulating the reserve and liquidity ratios of all banking and financial firms and for ensuring their ongoing compliance with them; for laying down the rules for all required financial reporting, including the provision of annual reports by the banking sector; for undertaking investigations into banking firms and their activities; and for the administration of banking firms and, where necessary, for overseeing their liquidation.

In pursuing its role from the earliest days, and especially its regulatory and supervisory functions, the BMA has always sought to pursue an open door policy where dialogue and persuasion take precedence over coercion and direction.

3
The Bahrain Monetary Agency

The legal identity

The Bahrain Monetary Agency (BMA) was established by Decree-Law No. 23 of 1973 and operates under the terms of that Law as an independent juristic personality headquartered in Manama, Kingdom of Bahrain. The activities of the BMA are funded by a special budget and are subjected to control solely under the terms of Decree Law No. 23, except in regard to all audits of its accounts and assets where other applicable laws take priority. When established the BMA had an authorised capital of BD1 million (US$2.7 million), one quarter paid. Today, the authorised capital is BD400 million (US$1.06 billion), BD200 million (US$530.5 million) paid.

The management and organisation of the BMA

The overall control of the BMA is vested in a Board of Directors comprising the Prime Minister, HH Shaikh Khalifa bin Salman Al Khalifa, the Minister of Finance and National Economy as his deputy and three other members who are appointed by Royal Decree for a three year term, which is renewable.

The Board of Directors has responsibility for the policies of the Agency, while the Governor administers and directs its day-to-day affairs, supported by the Deputy Governor. Both are assisted by the Strategic Planning, Legal, and Promotions and Media Units, whilst Internal Audit reports directly to them.

In 2002 the Chairman of the Board of Directors approved a new organisational structure for the Agency, which reflects the additional duties and responsibilities with which it is now vested as a single regulator of the whole banking and financial sector in Bahrain.

The structure

The new organisational structure of the Agency comprises four executive directors, each being responsible for one of Banking Operations, Corporate Services, Banking Supervision and Financial Institutions Supervision, with a number of directors with specific areas of responsibility reporting directly to them (see Exhibit 3.1).

Banking Operations

Banking Operations comprises three Directorates:

- currency issue;
- reserves management; and
- banking services.

The Currency Issue Directorate has responsibility for the national currency. The Reserves Management Directorate manages the Kingdom's official gold and foreign exchange reserves and the government's domestic debt, acts as the government's fiscal agent and meets the commercial banks' demand for US dollars whilst providing them with daily recommended exchange rates for defined currencies to be applied to customer transactions. Finally, the Banking Services' Directorate's major functions are:

- *debt management.* The issue, redemption and servicing of Treasury bills and development bonds on behalf of the government, in both conventional and Islamic formats denominated in local currency and US dollars;
- *discount window.* The provision of dinar liquidity to the local commercial banks through secondary market operations, including the discounting of conventional Treasury bills and government bonds denominated in dinars;
- *account maintenance.* The administration of the accounts of the commercial banks with the BMA, including the handling of all inter-bank fund transfers;

Exhibit 3.1: Organisational structure of the BMA

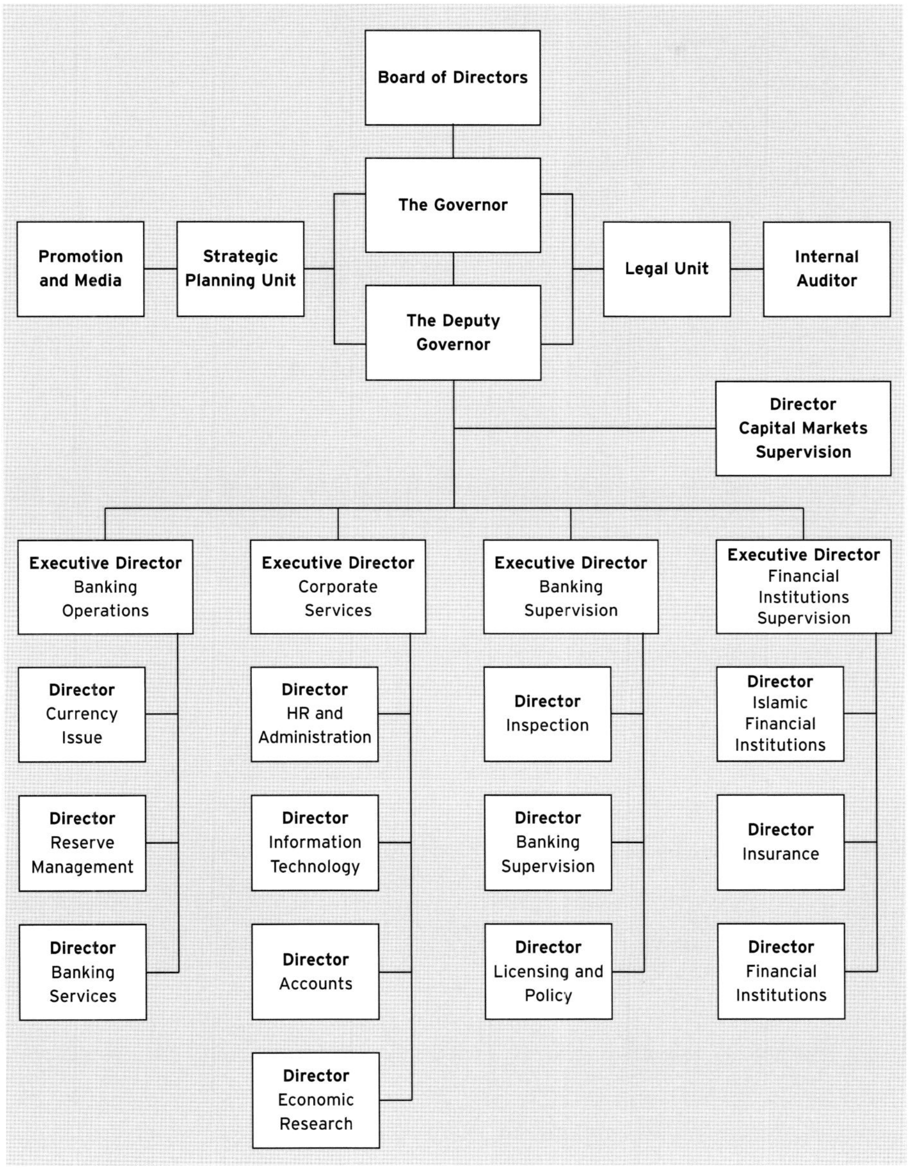

HE Abdulla Hasan Saif, the first Governor of the BMA, 1981–99

the banks' borrowings against dinar deposits with the BMA; and the granting of overdraft facilities to the banks by the BMA and their subsequent close monitoring; and

- *cheque clearing.* The operation of the local, fully automated cheques clearing house which has clearings twice a day.

Corporate Services

This division contains four Directorates, as follows:

- human resources and administration;
- information technology;
- accounts; and
- economic research.

Human Resources and Administration recruits, educates and trains all employees; manages all security-related activities; and provides general administrative support.

Economic Research collects, collates and analyses statistical information and prepares statistical analyses and reports on Bahrain's financial sector, including the BMA's Quarterly Statistical Bulletins and Annual Report, in addition to those required by such regional and international bodies as the GCC Secretariat, the International

Monetary Fund (IMF) and the Bank for International Settlements (BIS). Also, it participates in surveys coordinated by the IMF and every five years undertakes a review of the country's banking and financial policies for the World Trade Organisation (WTO).

The Accounts Directorate has specific responsibility for preparing the BMA's annual budget and statutory accounts, whilst information technology is the unit that ensures the availability of computer services across the BMA and is charged with the responsibility for maintaining the interbank settlement system (SWIFT); managing real-time gross settlement (RTGS), so enabling same day interbank settlements; automating all the BMA's activities, thereby enabling access worldwide by authorised staff and, where appropriate, by banks and the general public through either the BMA's intranet or via the BMA's website; and recommending relevant upgrades to the banking community so enhancing their capabilities with customers and their effectiveness in responding to the data requirements of the BMA.

Banking Supervision

This Division undertakes the regulation and supervision of conventional banks licensed by the BMA. It also contains two directorates – Licensing and Policy, and Inspections – which assist those supervising conventional banks as well as those supervising other types of licensees, who are located in the Financial Institutions Supervision Division (see below).

Banking supervision directorate analyses regulatory returns provided by licensed conventional banks and other available information, in order to monitor banking activity and performance. Also, the directorate interacts with management and Boards of Licensees, and responds to issues raised by the conventional banks. The Directorate works in co-operation with the Inspection Directorate to apply a risk-profiling methodology, which aims to help focus supervisory efforts on high-risk areas and to ensure consistency of approach across licensees.

The Licensing and Policy Directorate vets licence applications and develops new regulations. The directorate interfaces with applicants seeking a BMA licence and, once applications have been completed and reviewed, submits them to a Licensing Committee, composed of senior management from across supervisory directorates, for a formal decision.

Also within the directorate is the central risk unit, formed in September 1979, which monitors credit risks. All commercial banks cooperate with the unit by providing information on all borrowers with exposure above a defined amount. This information, whilst kept confidential on a bank-by-bank basis, once consolidated for each borrower may be accessed by authorised personnel in the banks to assist in lending decisions.

The Inspection directorate carries out on-site investigations, not solely of conventional banks but also of institutions supervised by the Financial Institutions Supervision Directorate (see below). The BMA first started on-site inspections in the late 1970s and today tailors these to the specific risk profile of a licensee. Examinations can cover a wide range of issues, but most focus on operational controls, compliance with internal procedures and regulatory requirements, and the quality of risk management and governance maintained by each bank or financial institution.

Financial Institutions Supervision Division

This Division was introduced in November 2002 as part of the internal reorganisation which took place after the assumption by the BMA of responsibility for insurance and capital markets supervision. The Division is responsible for the supervision of Islamic financial institutions, insurance companies and non-bank financial institutions.

The Financial Institutions Directorate monitors and supervises mutual funds, money brokers, moneychangers, investment managers, asset-backed products (SPVs) and conventional leasing companies.

The IFIs directorate monitors all such entities.

The Insurance supervision directorate monitors all insurance companies, brokers, agents and consultants, loss adjusters and actuaries. As at mid-2003, the Directorate was in the process of developing a completely new regulatory and supervisory framework for the insurance sector, for implementation in 2004.

Capital markets directorate, a wholly separate unit, reports directly to the Deputy Governor and fulfils the role of regulator and supervisor of the Bahrain Stock Exchange (BSE).

BMA objectives

The provision of a central banking service

Organisation of the currency issue

Bahrain has maintained its own domestic currency since 1965 but it was in 1979 that the BMA made its first issue of notes as a result of the passing of Legislative Decree

Bahrain Monetary Agency

No. 23, which included reference to the issuing of the 'First Currency Issue' (the 1965 issue having been made by the Bahrain Currency Board).

This new series of banknotes was issued in just four denominations – 10 dinars, five dinars, one dinar and a half dinar. The two smaller denominations of the earlier Bahrain Currency Board issue were not re-issued, nor were any coins. A 20 dinar note, which had been introduced in 1978, also became part of this issue. All the new notes, including the 20 dinar denomination, bore the name of the BMA.

In March 1993 the BMA issued a further set of banknotes known as the 'Second

Exhibit 3.2: Currency in circulation*, 1989–2000 (BD million)

Year	*BD20*	*BD10*	*BD5*	*BD1*	*BD0.5*	*Other notes*	*Coins*	*Total*
1989	68.2	14.9	2.5	4.1	1.1	-	3.3	94.1
1990	84.3	20.2	2.9	4.6	1.1	-	3.4	116.5
1991	80.6	16.7	3.1	5.1	1.3	-	3.8	110.6
1992	81.7	16.3	3.1	5.1	1.4	-	4.1	111.7
1993	86.7	16.3	3.4	5.3	1.4	-	4.4	117.5
1994	85.5	16.4	3.5	5.5	1.5	-	4.7	117.1
1995	85.4	16.2	3.6	5.8	1.6	-	5.0	117.6
1996	84.2	16.3	3.8	5.9	1.8	-	5.2	117.2
1997	91.5	18.0	3.7	5.2	1.4	-	2.9	122.7
1998	79.0	21.3	4.1	5.4	1.4	-	3.3	114.5
1999	120.1	23.4	4.6	.6.5	1.6	-	4.1	160.3
2000	110.9	23.5	5.5	7.6	0.8	-	5.9	154.2
2001	107.8	22.0	5.4	7.7	0.5	-	6.5	149.9
2002	127.5	25.0	5.9	8.1	0.5	-	7.2	174.2

* Notes and coins outside BMA

Source: Bahrain Monetary Agency, Economic research directorate, quarterly statistical abstracts.

Currency Issue', when a new set of coins was also introduced. These new notes were markedly different from the earlier issues, not only in design but also in their uniform size and, in the light of their introduction all those notes issued in 1979 remained in circulation for just three further years until they were fully withdrawn in March 1996, when a new half dinar note was added. The coins issued at this time were of the same denominations as the earlier issue with the exception of the one fils coin, which was withdrawn. By the end of 1996 the amount of currency in issue totalled BD117.2 million (US$310.9 million), of which BD102.9 million (US$272.9 million) was in circulation outside the banks.

In 1998, the BMA introduced the 'Second (New) Currency Issue', also comprising just four notes – 20 dinars, 10 dinars, five dinars and one dinar. Following the introduction of these notes, which were similar in design to the previous issue but with added security features, the issue of 1993 was progressively withdrawn, as was the half dinar note of 1996. By the end of 1998 the total currency in issue and circulation had fallen to BD114.5 million (US$306.1 million) and BD93.3 million (US$249.5 million) respectively.

As an exceptional case, the original 20 dinar note of this new issue was, in 1998, also withdrawn from circulation and ceased to be legal tender, being replaced later by an identical note in a different colour. This note was also soon to be superceded as, on the occasion of National Day, 16 December 2001, a new 20 dinar note was issued which was identical to its predecessor except for the addition on the obverse face of the note of a portrait of HM The King, Shaikh Hamad bin Isa Al Khalifa. Earlier, in January 2000, a new 500 fils coin had been introduced.

In 1999 the total currency in issue rose to BD160.3 million (US$428.6 million) but by the end of the succeeding year had reduced to BD154.2 million (US$409.0 million), with a further fall again the next year to BD149.9 million (US$397.6 million) although the amount of currency actually circulating in the marketplace – that is outside the banks – increased from BD113.0 million (US$299.7 million) at the end of 1999 to BD120.7 million (US$320.2 million) a year later and to BD122.9 million (US$326.0 million) at 31 December 2001. As at the end of 2002, the total in issue had reached BD174.2 million (US$465.8 million) with BD142 million (US$379.7 million) in circulation. A primary reason for the marked rise in circulation of the currency in 1999 and 2000 was the coincidence of the end of the Gregorian year with Ramadhan and its ensuing holiday, when families gift money, usually new notes, to their and their friends' children. Subsequent increases are directly interrelated with the progress made in the domestic economy and especially in the consumer sector.

A third issue of coins was introduced from 1 December 2002 reflecting Bahrain's new status as a kingdom. More than 14.2 million coins, worth BD1.644 million (US$4.396 million) were gradually released into the banking system by the BMA. The new coins, in denominations of 500 fils, 100 fils, 50 fils, 25 fils and 10 fils bear the name Kingdom of Bahrain, to replace the State of Bahrain, but are unchanged in size, design and denomination.

Maintaining the external value of the currency

The BMA was born into an environment of worldwide monetary instability brought about at the time by the devaluation of sterling, the substantial rise in the price of oil in 1973, worldwide inflation, the deficit financing of the Vietnam war by the United States, the de-linkage of the US dollar from gold and two subsequent devaluations of that currency.

It should be remembered, however, that enshrined in the law forming the BMA was the requirement that the Agency should maintain a foreign reserve of not less than 100 per cent of the value of the currency in circulation, a figure which could be reduced to 75 per cent if so decided by the Council of Ministers. This foreign reserve may comprise any or all of gold, convertible foreign currencies, SDRs (Special Drawing Rights) allocated to Bahrain by the IMF, the gold element of Bahrain's share in the IMF, foreign currency bills of exchange and promissory notes payable outside the Kingdom, Treasury bills of foreign governments in fully convertible currencies, bonds in convertible currencies guaranteed by foreign governments or international financial institutions with a maturity of up to 15 years and such other bonds as the BMA's Board of Directors determined, provided they were internationally negotiable, payable in convertible currencies and had less than 10 years to maturity from the date of acquisition. The existence of such a reserve proved markedly beneficial in maintaining the stability of the currency over the ensuing years.

From its earliest days in 1974, the BMA initiated a policy of publishing daily buying and selling rates for sterling and the dollar, thereby initiating a formal foreign exchange market in Bahrain. A year later, in 1975, three further currencies were added to those being quoted; the Kuwaiti dinar, the Deutschmark and the UAE dirham.

Exhibit 3.3: Bahrain's foreign exchange reserves, 1965-2002 (US$ million)

Year	*Currency market reserve less gold*	*Gold*	*Total reserves*
1965	22.7	-	22.7
1970	62.8	8.3	71.1
1975	289.5	6.1	295.6
1980	953.4	6.6	960.0
1985	1,659.7	6.6	1,666.3
1990	1,234.9	6.6	1,241.5
1995	1,279.9	6.6	1,286.5
1996	1,318.4	6.6	1,388.0
1997	1,290.3	6.6	1,296.5
1998	1,079.2	6.6	1,085.6
1999	1,369.0	6.6	1,375.6
2000	1,564.1	6.6	1,570.7
2001	1,684.0	6.6	1,690.6
2002	1,725.7	6.6	1,732.3

Source: IMF International Financial Statistics.

The exchange rate of the US dollar remained important however, as the country's main exports, aluminium and oil, were both priced in that currency. A decision was thus taken to fix the dinar/dollar rate within plus or minus 2.25 per cent of the gold parity rate, with rates for other currencies being calculated on the basis of market rates against the dollar. Thus, for many years to come, the US dollar selling rate remained at US$1 = BD0.3958. Then, on 26 January 1978, the decision was taken to peg the dinar to the SDR at the rate of BD0.47619 = SDR1, again with a margin of plus or minus 2.25 per cent. However, the dollar still remained the intervention currency.

As suggested, the 1970s were volatile times in world monetary markets with, in the latter years of the decade, yet further devaluations of the US dollar. In the light of this the Bahraini dinar was effectively revalued against the dollar at differing rates on a number of occasions – by 2 per cent in January 1978, which was when the dinar became pegged officially to the SDR; by 0.5 per cent in each of September and October of the same year; by 1 per cent in July 1979; 0.2 per cent in October and 0.5 per cent in November of that year; and by 0.2 per cent again in December 1980. For part of this period of extreme volatility all changes in the value of the dinar against the dollar were coordinated with Qatar and the United Arab Emirates (UAE) through an agreement to maintain fixed rates between their currencies, an arrangement which was to be discontinued in 1978.

The original margin against the SDR of plus or minus 2.25 per cent was widened in August 1978 to plus or minus 7.25 per cent. However, throughout the 1980s the dinar was effectively linked to the dollar and as that currency appreciated so the dinar/SDR rate exceeded the defined margin for a time. But when in 1986 the dollar was again devalued the dinar/SDR rate returned to within the defined parameters.

Since the early 1980s the daily buying and selling rates for the dinar against the dollar, quoted by the BMA to commercial banks, have remained unchanged at a buying rate of BD0.375 = US$1 and a selling rate of BD0.377 = US$1.

The relationship between the dinar and the SDR remained until December 2001 when the dinar formally became pegged to the US dollar, effectively confirming what had been the practice for many years. This change was in line with an agreement amongst the GCC States (Bahrain, Kuwait, Oman, Qatar, Saudi Arabia and the UAE) to prepare themselves for the unification of their currencies by 2010, and possibly as early as 2007.

Throughout the existence of the Bahraini dinar, the BMA's monetary policy of the fixed BD/US$ exchange rate has consistently been directed at the short-term regulation of domestic liquidity in order to ensure the stability of the exchange rate. Consequently, even during the extended period of currency turmoil, there has always been an open exchange and payments system in Bahrain with fully market-determined interest rates, albeit at levels recommended but not enforced by the BMA, whose founding objectives specifically included the right to 'set' interest rates. There is freedom in Bahrain to make transfers in foreign currencies, to import and export currency notes freely and to make capital transfers with the minimum of administrative control. Those controls that do exist are largely to ensure that financial institutions comply with money laundering regulations but, in practice also enable oversight and containment of large movements of capital across the Kingdom's borders. This absence of exchange controls and freedom of movement of funds, allied to the strength and stability of the dinar, have been wholly integral to Bahrain's success as an international financial centre.

Providing banking services to government and the banking industry

Although the BMA started operations during 1974, following issuance of its founding decree in 1973, the role of government banker, the depository of government funds or fiscal agent, the management of official foreign assets, other than the currency reserve, was left initially in the hands of the Ministry of Finance and National Economy. During 1975, however, the BMA was in a position to manage the government's gold and foreign exchange reserves on a fiduciary basis and to open a small deposit account for the government, albeit the bulk of the government's funds remained with the commercial banks.

Over the years the BMA has continued to manage the Kingdom's foreign exchange reserves both in-house and through major international financial institutions.

In supporting any deficit that might arise in the national budget, the Government issues and redeems Treasury bills and government bonds, which the BMA manages and, where applicable, pays on behalf of the Government any interest due. This is not always applicable: three recent issues, made in accordance with Islamic *Shari'a* law, do not bear interest but offer a yield-to-maturity based on the underlying value of the assets against which the bonds have been issued. In this case, the BMA acts solely as an agent of the government under the authority of the Ministry of Finance and National Economy.

After the BMA's first year of operation, the Issue Department, which was essentially the old Currency Board responsible for the national currency, ceased to be the sole active department and a number of important initiatives relevant to commercial banks were implemented. First, the Foreign Exchange Department was established whereby rates for a number of currencies were quoted on a daily basis; secondly, the Banking Department was set up to hold the accounts of the commercial banks; and thirdly a Banking Control Department was formed with the specific aim of gathering and processing statistics from the commercial banks and for monitoring developments in the banking sector.

The BMA subsequently assumed responsibility for the commercial banks' clearing house and instituted reserve requirements for commercial bank deposits of 5 per cent for those in local currency and 1 per cent for those in foreign currency, although the latter was abolished three years later. The Agency also took active steps to stabilise interest rates by recommending, although never imposing, deposit rates of differing maturities and seeking the banks' support in relating lending rates to them. In this latter regard, swap arrangements were also put in place to prevent foreign currency being purchased for despatch overseas in search of higher rates of interest, which could have destabilised the dinar. More recently, the BMA has sought to regulate bank liquidity through issuing and discounting Treasury bills and as a result has reduced such swap operations.

Sustaining and developing domestic financial markets

Regulation and supervision of the financial services industry

A primary function of the BMA is the regulation and supervision of banks and financial institutions. In August 2002 it was appointed the sole regulator of the financial sector, including the BSE and the insurance industry, which until this time had come under the authority of what is now the Ministry of Commerce.

Since its establishment, the BMA has always recognised that Bahrain's appeal as a destination for international financial institutions needed to be based on a stable, credible and transparent financial system, which would also ensure the financial community's ability to operate in accordance with internationally accepted practices. In ensuring the introduction and maintenance of such a system the BMA has been very successful, as evidenced not only by the number of financial institutions maintaining a presence in the Kingdom but also, and more importantly, by the solid reputation the international financial centre has attained.

Integral to its role, the BMA has the sole right to license participants in the financial sector, be they commercial, offshore or investment banks, investment and advi-

BMA Currency Museum

sory services companies, money brokers, moneychangers, commodity and bullion dealers and, more recently, stock brokers and participants in the insurance sector. Such participants may only operate with specifically licensed authority and usually must be legally established in Bahrain under the terms of the Commercial Companies Law.

Once present in the market, the activities, services and products of each institution are subject to the regulations and supervision imposed by the BMA in their entirety, with the Agency also ensuring their full compliance. In undertaking its obligations the

BMA collects annual registration fees; applies detailed reporting requirements specific to the business being established; encourages banks to set aside adequate provisions against bad and doubtful lending; and imposes and enforces an array of regulations to ensure close conformity of the sector with the latest internationally agreed criteria – which include the recommendations of the Basel Committee on Banking Supervision; the recommendations of the Financial Action Task Force on Money Laundering (FATF); the application of international accounting standards ; and, for Islamic institutions, the recommendations of the Accounting and Auditing Organization for Islamic Financial Institutions (AAOIFI). As a matter of course, the BMA also conducts inspections of financial institutions as part of its ongoing monitoring of licensees and ensures receipt of all necessary monthly, quarterly and annual returns.

Since 2002, when the BMA, became the single regulatory authority for the whole financial sector, substantial work has been initiated to enhance and improve every aspect of the regulatory and supervisory environment, including that for insurance and the stock exchange, to ensure Bahrain maintains its highly acclaimed and unique reputation as an international financial centre.

Ensuring adequate protection of the interests of consumers of financial products

Pivotal to the activities of the BMA is the desire to ensure not only the stability of the financial system as a whole but also the protection of depositors, policyholders and other consumers of financial services.

The BMA applies certain criteria in this regard, including the:

- approval and authorisation, in advance, of each and every collective investment scheme (mutual fund or unit trust) which may be established in, or marketed in, or from Bahrain;
- ongoing interaction with all financial institutions in Bahrain to ensure the application of prudence in the fulfilment of all their activities;
- introduction in 1993 of a depositor protection scheme under which small depositors enjoy protection against the failure of a commercial bank;
- registration of all management staff working in the sector to ensure the quality, competence, professionalism and integrity of the sector;
- compliance of all financial institutions with defined reporting requirements to enable the BMA to supervise their activities;
- introduction of a code of conduct applicable to dealing practices in brokerages

and banks in accordance with agreements between the brokers, the BMA and the Bahrain Society of Bankers;

- imposition of a requirement for guarantee from moneychangers as a guard, in part at least, against non-payment of bank drafts on presentation;
- investigation of all potential participants in the investment and financial advisory services sector to ensure their reputation and standing prior to accepting their applications to operate in Bahrain.

These activities have brought a sense of security to local and foreign investors alike in what has become a highly competitive environment providing a wide array of services comparable with those available in other major financial centres around the world. In ensuring continuity and security in safeguarding the financial system in the country the BMA constantly seeks to keep abreast of the latest regulatory developments worldwide for implementation at the earliest opportune moment.

The promotion of Bahrain as an international financial centre

The creation and maintenance of relationships with international financial institutions

From the earliest days of banking in Bahrain foreign institutions have been wholly integral to the banking and financial environments. In the 1970s, at a time of increasing wealth throughout the oil-producing states of the region, international bankers increasingly sought to attain business from and within the region.

At the same time, the BMA was in the process of being established and, having made the decision that the domestic banking sector was sufficiently well-served, took the initiative to establish the country as an offshore centre. To achieve this, it was necessary early on to formulate a set of regulations conducive to the encouragement of new entrants to the market and direct approaches to banks and financial institutions worldwide to increase their awareness of the opportunity that now existed. Given the international banking community's recognition of potential opportunities in the Gulf States, arising from increased oil revenues, and the reputation that Bahrain had already earned as a stable location, well-placed for access to the other states in the region, there was a ready audience.

Furthermore, there was also an increasing demand for high quality, professional banking and financial services in the region following the demise of Beirut in 1975, the general dearth of such services within the GCC's financial sector and the absence of a meaningful alternative within the Middle East. So, the possibility of Bahrain becoming that financial centre had a clear appeal.

Once Bahrain had become established as the location of choice for banking in the region, the BMA had by necessity to fulfil the vital role of ensuring the attainment and maintenance of a properly regulated and supervised financial environment. The BMA's success in this regard was of itself a subsequent incentive to financial institutions to make Bahrain their regional base.

In the light of its early success in attracting international commercial banks, the BMA progressively introduced further licences of specific interest to the international financial community for establishing various other offshore banking institutions, including investment banks, representative offices, foreign exchange and money brokers and providers of investment and financial services, thereby ensuring the availability of a broad spread of financial activities. The number of countries represented amongst the financial entities now established in Bahrain covers a wide geographical area; from the United States and Europe to Brazil, Japan and Turkey. This too was a direct result of the BMA's intention to ensure widespread knowledge of the country as an international financial centre and to ensure tangible recognition of the global nature of that centre.

Over the years, the financial sector has developed and changed in line with economic prosperity in the region. The BMA has maintained its faith in the strength of the sector, recognising its importance to the economy of Bahrain and its contribution to GDP. Consequently, the BMA continues to seek new opportunities. For example, it has ensured Bahrain is the major centre in the Middle East for Islamic banking and finance, with two-thirds of all IFIs in the region now based in the country. With the introduction of new rules and regulations for the sector during 2002, it is anticipated the sector will grow exponentially as the much anticipated demand for such services increases.

The BMA's success in attracting international financial entities to the country has in part been born out of its ability to be innovative and pro-active, but has also been a result of its attention to detail and the maintenance of high standards of regulation and supervision, which have in themselves served to enhance Bahrain's status as the premier provider of financial services in the Middle East.

Ensuring the reputation of the financial centre is adequately and expressly promoted in all major financial markets

To sustain interest in Bahrain as an international financial centre and to ensure continued recognition of its reputation, the BMA has taken a number of important steps. The first has been to cooperate with the international regulatory community. In so doing the Agency has ensured not only that the Kingdom is fully compliant with the requirements or recommendations of the IMF, the BIS and the FATF, but also that the international community is fully conversant with the fact that Bahrain enjoys full recognition for such compliance.

To achieve the latter, the Governor of the BMA, Shaikh Ahmed bin Mohammed Al Khalifa, as well as other members of his senior management team, have participated directly in promoting Bahrain in international conferences, forums, seminars and other gatherings of financial leaders and companies, such as those held under the auspices of the World Bank, the IMF and the World Economic Forum. The BSE has also been directly involved in the country's promotion, as have the Bankers' Society of Bahrain, the Bahrain Institute of Banking and Finance (BIBF) and the Bahrain Insurance Association all of which, under the terms of their existence, are obligated to promote Bahrain. In addition, numerous economic and finance-related conferences are held in Bahrain supported by the BMA as organiser, sponsor or participant. The publication of articles on Bahrain in relevant financial journals has also served to maintain the BMA's profile worldwide as well as highlight the quality of the regulatory environment.

The BMA cooperates closely with other monetary authorities worldwide on a host of issues relevant to their activities and to those of their banking and financial communities. Bahrain has maintained especially close relations with the authorities in London, New York, Hong Kong, Singapore and, with particular regard to Islamic banking matters, Malaysia, as well as with those within the GCC. Such cooperation has been of vital importance in recent years as governments around the globe have sought to prevent money laundering and the financing of terrorist activities. The BMA's involvement has been fully instrumental in ensuring recognition of the country's desire to be identified as an international financial centre that not only supports but abides by the most stringent requirements of the international community, resulting in recognition by its peers as the leader in its field within the Gulf. However, in the final analysis, it is the professional competence of the institutions and the personal probity of the staff employed in them that attract international banks and financial institutions to Bahrain.

Taking on the role of single regulator for the financial sector

In August 2002 the BMA became the single integrated regulator in Bahrain covering all of banking and finance, insurance and capital markets, representing another first for the

Gulf region. This change in the regulatory structure reflects the government's strong commitment to the continuous development of Bahrain as an international financial centre.

Integral to the BMA's decision to pursue this role are three prime considerations:

- sectoral regulators worldwide are being overtaken by the evolution of financial markets and their participants, which has served to blur what were previously distinct financial sectors and has seen growth in conglomerates;
- integrated regulators are better placed to be more effective and efficient than a number of sectoral and functional regulators;
- integrated regulators are better placed to achieve greater regulatory consistency across the whole financial sector.

The key advantages for Bahrain lie in the latter two considerations – greater effectiveness and efficiency and consistency. As a small country, the availability of specialist skills tends to be limited. So, bringing together the regulation of the whole financial sector under one entity enables better use of those resources more cost effectively. Most importantly, however, the move to a single regulator seeks to ensure the maintenance of Bahrain's position as a reputable destination for international banks and financial institutions by building on the Kingdom's existing regulatory reputation fully cognisant of the need to change to meet evolving standards and risks.

4
Domestic banking

Commercial banks

From humble beginnings in the 1920s, commercial banking in Bahrain has grown commensurately with developments in the national economy. Thus, there was rapid growth in the number of commercial banks in the late 1960s and early 1970s, when the country was beginning to enjoy enhanced revenues. However, in the mid- to late-1970s the BMA felt the need to limit the number of commercial banks and so just four commercial banking licences were issued between then and 2001, these being Bahrain Islamic Bank in 1978, The Bahraini Saudi Bank in 1983, Grindlays Bahrain Bank in 1984 and Faisal Bank in 1992. In 2001, four banks, all from within the GCC,

Al Baraka Islamic Bank

NBB Tower

were licensed to operate. This recent licensing of GCC-based banks has arisen, at least in part, from intra-GCC agreements to allow institutions based in one member state to operate in another. In 2002 there was a further increase in the number of banks licensed to operate: BankMuscat (following its purchase of the assets and the single branch of ABN AMRO Bank), National Bank of Kuwait and The Housing Bank for Trade and Finance, registered in Jordan. As at end May 2003, there were 23 full commercial banks operating in the Kingdom, of which seven were locally incorporated (see Exhibit 4.1) and four operated according to Islamic principles: AlBaraka

Exhibit 4.1: Commercial banks operating in Bahrain, as at end May 2003

Bank	*Country of incorporation*	*Established*	*Number of branches*
AlBaraka Islamic Commercial Bank EC	Bahrain	2001	1
Ahli United Bank (Bahrain) BSC*	Bahrain	2001	15
Arab Bank plc	Jordan	1960	4
BNP Paribas**	France	1975	1
Bahrain Islamic Bank BSC	Bahrain	1978	7
Bahraini Saudi Bank BSC	Bahrain	1983	6
Bank Melli Iran	Iran	1970	2
Bank Saderat Iran	Iran	1974	1
Bank of Bahrain and Kuwait BSC	Bahrain	1971	20
BankMuscat SAOG	Oman	2002	1
Citibank N.A.	United States	1969	2
HSBC Bank Middle East	Jersey	1944	4
Habib Bank Limited	Pakistan	1968	3
Kuwait Finance House - Bahrain BSC	Bahrain	2001	1
National Bank of Abu Dhabi	UAE	2001	1
National Bank of Bahrain BSC	Bahrain	1957	25
National Bank of Kuwait	Kuwait	2002	1
Rafidain Bank	Iraq	1969	1
Saudi National Commercial Bank	Saudi Arabia	2002	1
Shamil Bank of Bahrain EC (Islamic Bankers)***	Bahrain	1993	5
Standard Chartered Bank PLC	United Kingdom	1920	5
The Housing Bank for Trade and Finance	Jordan	2002	1
United Bank Limited	Pakistan	1969	3

* Incorporating both AlAhli Commercial Bank (established in 1977) and Commercial Bank of Bahrain (formerly Grindlays Bahrain Bank, established in 1984).

** Formerly Paribas. Changed in May 2000 after the merger of BNP and Paribas (France).

*** Formerly Faisal Islamic Bank of Bahrain.

Source: BMA, Licensing and Information Unit, 29 May 2003.

Islamic Commercial Bank EC; Bahrain Islamic Bank BSC; Kuwait Finance House (Bahrain) BSC ©; and Shamil Bank of Bahrain EC (Islamic Bankers).

Exhibit 4.2: Commercial banks - consolidated balance sheet - assets, 1968-76 (BD million)

Year end	*Reserves cash*	*Reserves balances with BMA*	*Advances/ credits*	*Foreign assets*	*Balance with local banks*	*Other assets*	*Contra A/Cs*	*Total*
1968	1.55	-	18.14	24.75	0.31	1.37	8.95	55.07
1969	1.37	-	23.85	23.05	0.38	1.67	11.24	61.56
1970	1.20	-	24.73	27.23	0.89	1.60	17.17	72.82
1971	1.64	-	37.57	38.18	0.67	4.46	16.97	99.49
1972	1.51	-	53.13	46.76	0.98	5.81	21.48	129.67
1973	1.24	-	76.36	45.15	6.83	15.80	42.69	188.07
1974	2.42	-	122.00	98.88	13.98	14.44	54.92	306.64
1975	2.38	22.87	162.10	160.59	35.90	13.54	89.71	487.09
1976	3.58	34.87	271.47	189.85	38.96	23.54	192.15	754.42

Source: BMA Quarterly Statistical Bulletin - September 1977.

Economic growth boosts commercial banks

Development of the commercial banks over the years has taken place hand-in-hand with economic growth, whilst also enjoying strong, ongoing support from the BMA. As the government sought economic diversification, so new opportunities arose which necessitated the close involvement of the local banking community. In the late 1960s, Aluminium Bahrain was the basis for industrial diversification of the economy to be followed over time by a number of other major projects able to generate export revenue and/or to provide feedstock for downstream industries. But equally as important were the events which led to the sharp rise in world oil prices in 1973, which proved so beneficial for all the oil-producing states in the region, both in terms of revenues for their governments and in terms of the impact they had on the development of their national economies.

In Bahrain the commercial banks became clear beneficiaries of these increased resources. In 1968 the balance sheets of the commercial banks indicated total assets of just BD55.07 million (US$146.1 million) but by the end of 1976, just eight years later, this figure had grown to BD754.42 million (US$2 billion), with the major part of that growth occurring in the last four years of the period, when assets actually quadrupled (see Exhibit 4.2). Private and government deposits combined amounted to BD40.23 million (US$106.7 million) in 1968 but had reached BD338.3 million (US$897.3 mil-

Exhibit 4.3: Commercial banks – consolidated balance sheet – liabilities, 1968-76

Year end	*Private deposits*	*Government deposits*	*Foreign liabilities*	*Due to local banks*	*Capital and reserves*	*Other liabilities*	*Contra A/Cs*	*Total*
1968	28.54	11.69	2.43	0.32	0.95	2.19	8.95	55.07
1969	31.21	8.96	5.89	0.37	1.46	2.43	11.24	50.32
1970	37.58	8.23	4.49	1.02	1.20	3.13	17.17	72.82
1971	51.91	11.78	10.01	0.33	1.96	6.53	16.97	99.49
1972	64.07	13.67	17.26	0.95	3.45	8.79	21.48	129.67
1973	84.73	11.30	23.05	6.49	6.21	13.60	42.69	188.07
1974	128.95	32.05	60.85	12.82	7.61	9.44	54.92	306.64
1975	160.20	50.51	129.74	35.90	9.39	11.64	89.71	487.09
1976	269.61	68.67	154.24	38.96	14.17	16.62	192.15	754.42

Source: BMA Quarterly Statistical Bulletin – September 1977.

lion) eight years later, an average year-on-year growth of 93 per cent (see Exhibit 4.3). Over the same period, loans and advances had grown by 1,376 per cent, or 172 per cent average year-on-year, from BD18.14 million (US$48.1 million) to BD271.5 million (US$720.1 million), indicating the rapid pace of economic activity and the large demand for credit for the new industrial enterprises, real estate and construction in general at that time. Later in the 1970s, the conventional commercial banks were to be joined by a number of Islamic commercial banks, the first of which, Bahrain Islamic Bank, began operations in 1978.

Licensing requirements

For a full commercial banking licence to be issued, a legal minimum paid-in capital of BD0.5 million is required but in practice at least BD7.54 million (US$20 million) is necessary; primary liquid assets should not be less than 25 per cent of total deposit liabilities; and a minimum daily cash reserve balance must be maintained with the BMA amounting to 5 per cent of Bahraini dinar deposits from non-bank customers and dinar certificates of deposit. Islamic banking and finance is dealt with in full in Chapter 6, but it should be noted here that the minimum capital requirements for Islamic commercial banks are the same as for the conventional banks and funds

Exhibit 4.4: Commercial banks - consolidated balance sheet - assets, 1977-86 (BD million)

Year end	*Reserves cash*	*Reserves balances with BMA*	*Advances/ Credits*	*Foreign Assets*	*Balance with local banks*	*Other Assets*	*Contra A/Cs*	*Total*
1977	3.02	22.34	315.34	223.55	38.03	36.64	186.11	825.03
1978	5.46	28.48	341.39	243.79	27.96	45.34	211.14	903.57
1979	3.90	32.99	395.20	236.67	21.96	56.03	185.03	931.78
1980	3.18	34.58	454.15	319.96	26.83	62.23	238.89	1,139.82
1981	3.45	37.35	495.35	343.12	15.44	65.20	279.94	1,239.85
1982	3.94	49.98	568.55	358.07	18.38	71.25	455.71	1,525.88
1983	5.11	31.15	630.36	470.05	12.77	78.61	431.69	1,659.74
1984	5.30	34.69	727.82	435.82	25.01	99.00	544.00	1,871.64
1985	6.44	50.02	677.50	586.79	30.51	105.32	515.21	1,971.79
1986	5.91	41.47	678.94	694.62	22.07	109.05	532.90	2,084.96

Source: BMA Quarterly Statistical Bulletin - December 1986.

placed with such banks are restricted to 20 times their capital and reserves. As to liquidity requirements, the BMA anticipates both conventional and Islamic banks should have primary liquid assets of not less than one quarter of total on-balance sheet funds; that exposure to any one client will not exceed 15 per cent of the bank's capital and reserves; and that total financings to all directors collectively must not exceed 30 per cent of those same capital and reserves.

The BMA also imposes a daily reserve requirement on all commercial banks, whether conventional or Islamic, of 5 per cent of local currency funds from non-banks. Most importantly, all Islamic commercial banks, like all other Islamic financial institutions (IFIs), must have religious advisory boards, who are independent of the bank's main board of directors and from whom advice on the compliance of the banks themselves and their activities with Shari'a law must be sought on an ongoing basis and especially prior to the introduction of new products or services.

The rate of growth in assets seen during the period 1973 to 1976 was not to be repeated in the following years as the pace of domestic economic activity slowed considerably. In 1977 the banks' assets grew by only 14 per cent year-on-year and in both 1978 and 1979 by just 8 per cent a year (see Exhibit 4.4). In 1980, however, the rate of growth of assets had again increased to 16 per cent year-on-year, reflecting higher eco-

Exhibit 4.5: Commercial banks - consolidated balance sheet - liabilities, 1977-86 (BD million)

Year end	*Private deposits*	*Government deposits*	*Foreign liabilities*	*Due to local banks*	*Capital and reserves*	*Other liabilities*	*Contra A/Cs*	*Total*
1977	311.73	49.02	197.75	38.04	21.50	20.88	186.11	825.03
1978	358.20	66.87	191.80	27.96	24.32	23.28	211.14	903.57
1979	361.97	50.77	235.79	21.96	34.66	41.61	185.03	931.78
1980	465.75	84.96	236.01	26.83	42.56	44.82	238.89	1,139.82
1981	667.20	59.88	122.83	15.43	62.73	31.84	279.94	1,239.85
1982	709.75	58.91	125.20	18.38	122.28	35.65	455.71	1,525.88
1983	769.58	114.10	149.89	12.77	137.59	44.12	431.69	1,659.74
1984	749.60	240.48	104.99	25.92	130.89	75.76	544.00	1,871.64
1985	824.33	242.62	127.65	30.50	167.79	63.69	515.21	1,971.79
1986	805.19	270.82	161.61	22.10	252.73	49.61	532.90	2,084.96

Source: BMA Quarterly Statistical Bulletin - December 1986.

Exhibit 4.6 Commercial banks - consolidated balance sheet - assets, 1987-95 (BD million)

Year end	*Reserves cash*	*Reserves balances with BMA*	*Advances/ credits*	*Foreign assets*	*Balance with local banks*	*Other assets*	*Contra A/Cs*	*Total*
1987	6.45	47.62	713.12	694.34	20.83	138.70	636.25	2,257.31
1988	9.67	38.98	606.56	855.88	20.05	142.83	510.98	2,184.95
1989	9.31	44.14	610.13	1,170.47	28.55	191.85	514.45	2,568.90
1990	11.27	185.44	635.82	941.90	7.07	89.77	436.18	2,307.45
1991	11.63	129.87	595.23	1,069.52	33.34	175.66	571.36	2,586.61
1992	11.82	104.73	654.45	1,004.90	35.34	236.92	614.70	2,662.86
1993	13.55	59.68	789.48	1,140.91	31.77	226.16	1,038.35	3,299.90
1994	11.62	54.70	882.99	1,403.57	25.23	240.82	967.46	3,586.39
1995	14.32	110.32	924.70	1,296.46	32.44	244.47	1,078.82	3,701.54

Source: BMA Quarterly Statistical Bulletin - December 1995.

nomic activity in the country in the wake of the 1979/1980 oil price increases. The revolution in Iran in 1979 had only a minimal impact on Bahrain's banking community but the subsequent Iraq-Iran war, which persisted from 1980 to 1990, despite a cease-fire agreed in 1988, created substantial uncertainty in the Gulf. This did affect banks and financial institutions in Bahrain but not to a major extent as further growth was seen during that period.

Exhibit 4.7: Commercial banks - consolidated balance sheet - liabilities, 1987-95 (BD million)

Year end	*Private deposits*	*Government deposits*	*Foreign liabilities*	*Due to local banks*	*Capital and reserves*	*Other liabilities*	*Contra A/Cs*	*Total*
1987	884.39	318.62	146.72	20.78	201.92	48.63	636.25	2,257.31
1988	923.23	334.55	160.13	20.01	172.34	63.71	510.98	2,184.95
1989	967.66	448.13	326.19	28.65	169.48	114.34	514.45	2,568.90
1990	825.48	511.12	286.82	7.10	132.81	107.94	436.18	2,307.45
1991	1,022.73	461.01	285.73	33.18	111.88	100.72	571.36	2,586.61
1992	1,067.63	362.32	333.98	35.26	155.69	93.28	614.70	2,662.86
1993	1,127.64	372.74	458.49	31.78	169.10	101.80	1,038.35	3,299.90
1994	1,201.87	455.59	629.52	25.17	194.58	112.20	967.46	3,586.39
1995	1,294.25	462.16	522.66	41.44	185.47	116.74	1,078.82	3,701.54

Source: BMA Quarterly Statistical Bulletin - December 1995.

Indeed, balance sheet footings did show growth between 1987 and 2001 (see Exhibit 4.6) but at a much slower pace than had been the case earlier. The end of 1990 was a marked exception to this growth pattern due in large part to the events leading up to the Gulf War in early 1991, which had such an adverse affect on the confidence of the international banking community over the short term.

Commercial lending

The commercial banks in Bahrain play an important role in the economic development of the country by extending loans and advances to satisfy the needs of those operating in every sector of the economy – be it the government, by way of budgetary support, or the private sector, by extending facilities to support and enhance their businesses or their private lives.

Over the 35 years covered by these figures, advances and credits and, more recently, private non-bank assets have reflected clearly the overall development of Bahrain's economy. Growth was steady over the initial 18 years as the country derived maximum benefits from enhanced revenues; major industrial projects were constructed and came into production; the real estate market expanded as new businesses came to Bahrain requiring both commercial and residential facilities; and the banking sector itself saw rapid expansion. In 1985, however, there was a marked downturn in lending as eco-

Exhibit 4.8: Commercial banks - consolidated balance sheet - assets, 1996-2002 (BD million)

Domestic assets

Year end	*Cash*	*BMA*	*Banks*	*Private non-banks*	*Government loans*	*Government securities*	*Other*	*Domestic assets total*	*Foreign assets*	*Total assets*
1996	14.3	84.7	446.9	954.7	17.5	149.1	63.9	1,731.0	961.5	2,692.5
1997	18.1	108.5	556.4	1,074.3	51.0	121.1	127.4	2,056.7	1,076.5	3,133.2
1998	21.2	68.2	553.4	1,160.0	68.3	159.2	63.6	2,094.0	1,189.7	3,283.7
1999	47.3	106.5	613.7	1,302.6	100.9	222.9	69.2	2,463.1	1,282.4	3,745.5
2000	33.5	105.6	566.9	1,380.5	100.8	221.5	73.4	2,482.2	1,285.9	3,768.1
2001	27.0	150.8	628.8	1,410.9	116.1	217.4	79.9	2,630.9	1,251.3	3,882.2
2002	32.2	172.0	542.3	1,606.6	108.4	203.3	82.8	2,747.6	1,273.9	4,021.5

Source: BMA Quarterly Statistical Bulletin - December 2002.

Exhibit 4.9: Commercial banks - consolidated balance sheet - liabilities, 1996-2002 (BD million)

Domestic liabilities

Year end	*BMA*	*Banks*	*Private non-banks*	*Government*	*Other*	*Capital and reserves*	*Domestic liabilities* total	Foreign liabilities	Total liabilities
1996	46.6	135.5	1,365.0	433.3	128.8	191.5	2,300.7	391.9	2,692.6
1997	42.8	176.5	1,481.4	443.1	194.6	199.4	2,537.9	595.3	3,133.2
1998	51.8	210.1	1,750.0	409.9	34.7	254.9	2,711.5	572.3	3,283.7
1999	117.5	227.3	1,798.8	432.2	43.5	259.4	2,878.7	866.8	3,745.5
2000	39.5	303.0	2,013.9	437.9	50.7	294.1	3,139.1	629.0	3,768.1
2001	31.9	315.3	2,195.0	427.5	44.1	311.9	3,325.7	556.5	3,882.2
2002	44.3	233.1	2,314.1	440.7	54.2	357.5	3,443.9	577.6	4,021.5

Source: BMA Quarterly Statistical Bulletin - December 2002.

nomic confidence fell following a slump in oil revenues. It was to be another 10 years before private sector borrowing reached the same level again, since when it has continued a steady rise through to the end of 2002.

A primary objective laid down for the BMA at its inception was to 'control and direct bank credit so as to realise the objectives of the economic policy of the government'. However, in practice, and in accordance with the government's desire for free

Exhibit 4.10: Commercial bank loans and advances by economic sector, 1979-2002 (BD million)

Year	*Manufact-uring*	*Agriculture, fisheries, and dairies*	*Const-ruction*	*Trade*	*Transport*	*Others **	*Total business*	*Government*	*Personal*	*Total*
1979	51.8	1.7	153.1	96.2	16.5	15.4	334.7	19.4	41.1	395.2
1982	38.9	1.2	166.2	175.9	12.8	28.4	423.4	23.9	121.3	568.6
1985	96.4	0.6	180.3	168.1	11.3	39.5	496.2	34.4	147.3	677.9
1988	75.7	1.2	160.4	118.1	24.0	26.9	406.3	61.3	139.0	606.6
1991	113.5	1.7	91.4	118.2	30.6	57.7	413.1	15.0	167.2	595.3
1994	140.2	2.2	126.7	166.4	28.1	90.5	554.1	35.7	293.1	882.9
1997	157.6	5.8	144.5	223.3	19.7	102.6	653.5	51.0	380.3	1,084.8
1998	189.4	5.9	139.5	259.2	15.9	88.5	698.4	64.1	410.5	1,173.0
1999	210.1	4.1	158.7	278.8	-	129.7	781.4	100.9	467.6	1,349.9
2000	199.4	4.6	170.9	309.4	30.6	106.3	821.2	100.8	499.5	1,421.5
2001	221.5	6.5	168.5	284.8	22.4	97.1	800.8	116.1	531.7	1,448.6
2002	255.7	5.9	176.9	299.6	13.2	91.4	842.7	106.4	678.7	1,629.8

* Others includes mining and quarrying, non-bank financial and hotels and restaurants.

Source: BMA Quarterly Statistical Bulletin, December 2002.

market policies to prevail, whatever activity the BMA has taken in this regard, and the indications are such activities have been minimal, has always been on an unofficial basis during the four or five meetings held each year by the Governor of the BMA and the Bankers' Society of Bahrain.

Despite the absence of such direction, the local commercial banks have succeeded in providing support over the years across every active economic sector, but especially to trade, manufacture, construction, real estate and the government. Overall, however, the major direction for all advances and loans has been to the personal sector which, over many years, has been the beneficiary of in excess of 30 per cent of the total outstanding loans and advances at any one time (see Exhibit 4.10), and reached over 40 per cent in 2002.

These figures evidence an overall growth of 266.6 per cent over the 22 years covered, which implies an average annual rate of growth of 12.1 per cent. This is a not inconsiderable rate of growth but when analysed in the context of Bahrain, where funding is available predominantly from the local commercial banks, the figure is not excessive. That said, the BMA does maintain a watching brief over bank lending through analysis of the regular returns required from the commercial banks and, as and when necessary, inspections. Should action be necessary, the BMA may intervene to seek to prevent the possibility of excessive or inappropriate lending, as it did on a rare occasion with regards to construction lending in 1976.

As an international financial centre, Bahrain has been able to derive maximum benefit from exposure to the latest financial products and services, thereby enhancing the capabilities of the indigenous commercial banks and enabling their active participation in major financings both in Bahrain and elsewhere within the Gulf States. Such activities have frequently been in close association with international financial institutions based in Bahrain or with their parent companies in their countries of origin. The involvement of the commercial banks has been evident also in the development of the Bahrain Stock Exchange (BSE) through the provision of liquid funds and the issuance of marketable securities.

Employment in the commercial banking sector

Integral to the growth of the commercial banking sector has been the development of indigenous personnel. Training has been fully encouraged by the BMA with the primary aims of ensuring the employability and professionalism of Bahraini workers. Success in this regard is borne out by the figures which show clearly that for many years Bahrainis have comprised 85 per cent or more of total employees in the sector. The commercial banks are the major employer within the banking sector, with 48 per cent of all employees in the sector (excluding non-bank financial sector employees) and 44 per cent of all employees in banking and finance.

Specialist banks

There are two specialist banks operating in Bahrain, both locally incorporated and established by the government to fulfil specific development and social tasks. These are the Bahrain Development Bank and The Housing Bank.

Bahrain Development Bank (BDB)

BDB was incorporated by Amiri Decree No. 19 of 1991, with an authorised capital of BD25 million (US$66.3 million), of which BD10 million (US$26.5 million) has been

Exhibit 4.11: Bahrain Development Bank, loan and equity approvals, during 1999, 2000 and 2001 (BD '000s)

	1999		*2000*		*2001*	
Sector	*No.*	*Value*	*No.*	*Value*	*No.*	*Value*
Manufacturing	24	1,809	26	1,620	13	3,117
Health	3	238	4	541	5	1,600
Tourism	1	97	4	325	1	260
Education	2	54	4	204	2	63
Others	3	117	6	189	13	1,954
Fisheries	-	-	123	1,045	155	1,265
Agriculture	-	-	-	-	31	105
Total	**33**	**2,810**	**167**	**3,924**	**22**	**8,364**

Source: Bahrain Development Bank Annual Report 2001.

issued and fully paid. When formed, the BDB's shares were held by the Government of Bahrain, the Pension Fund Commission and the General Organisation for Social Insurance (GOSI) (2 million shares each), and the National Imports and Exports Company (1 million shares), as well as by local banks and private sector investors, who held the remaining 3 million shares in issue. However, following a reform of its capital structure in 1996, the BDB has been effectively nationalised as now it is wholly owned by the first three of the investors named above. This change was brought about by the Government's desire to broaden the Bank's client base, to enhance employment opportunities for Bahraini nationals, to assist in the enhancement of the level of exports and to bring added value to the country's economy.

The BDB opened its doors in January 1992 with the principle aim of providing a platform on which to build and diversify the national economy by bringing together capital, technology and skills with local entrepreneurs. In fulfilling this role the BDB's defined objectives were to:

- contribute to the diversification of productive activities in the country through the promotion of investment in commercial, industrial and service activities;
- attract foreign investment;
- mobilise technical and technological skills to the benefit of development projects;

- participate in the ownership of both new and existing projects; and
- provide loans, guarantees, equity, lease and export finance as well as consultancy services.

In pursuing these objectives, special attention was to be given to small and medium enterprises (SMEs), for whom the BDB sought to provide a range of products and services including short, medium and long-term loans, project finance, fixed asset loans and guarantees, working capital and bridging loans, lease finance, export finance, equity investment, management consultancy services and specialised support appropriate to small businesses. Project creation and development assistance have also been prime elements of the services offered.

In October 2000, the government transferred management of its agricultural lending programme to the BDB and, during the same year, a Business Incubator Centre began operation in close proximity to the location of the new port in Hidd offering work areas for small businesses to initiate their activities. Incorporated into the centre are centralised support facilities and business counselling services, the latter provided under the management of UNIDO.

Between 1992 and the end of 2001, 592 loans and equity investments with a value of BD35 8 million (US$95.7 million) had been approved. Of these, 220 with a value of BD8.4 million (US$22.45 million) were granted in 2001, with 155 loans being made to fishermen to purchase boats and equipment. Other borrowers from the BDB have included entrepreneurs and companies in the fields of manufacturing, tourism, private healthcare, private education, information technology and agriculture, with most approvals in 2001 being to entities in the first three sectors mentioned.

In order to ensure the ready availability of technologically trained staff, the BDB has taken the initiative to establish the Bahrain Institute of Technology as a wholly owned subsidiary. A close relationship has been developed with the Ministry of Labour and Social Affairs for the provision of training members of the local workforce.

A further role filled by the BDB is that of national agent for the Jeddah-based Islamic Development Bank's (IDB) Longer-Term Trade Finance Programme. Under this scheme, local manufacturers receive funding for their exports to other member states of the Organization of Islamic Conference (OIC). The first participation in this scheme took place in 1996 since when a number of exporting companies have derived benefit from the programme.

Exhibit 4.12: The Housing Bank - loans open, 1980-2002 (BD)

Year	*Offline* accounts*	*Value*	*Open* accounts*	*Value*	*Total opened*	*Total value*
1980	241	2,548,540	441	5,539,570	682	8,088,110
1981	193	3,071,938	353	6,597,300	546	9,669,238
1982	263	3,159,360	567	8,858,140	830	12,017,500
1983	199	2,166,304	416	5,379,580	615	7,545,884
1984	101	1,342,310	324	5,261,000	425	6,603,310
1985	129	2,043,200	329	5,438,700	458	7,481,900
1986	81	1,237,900	318	6,021,220	399	7,259,120
1987	88	1,629,200	400	8,323,550	488	9,952,750
1988	92	1,599,000	447	8,639,170	539	10,238,170
1989	123	2,199,200	671	14,395,960	794	16,595,160
1990	72	1,129,575	454	8,696,400	526	9,825,975
1991	73	1,365,000	488	9,203,900	561	10,568,900
1992	70	1,173,300	608	11,921,050	678	13,094,350
1993	48	689,600	485	7,679,600	533	8,369,200
1994	26	537,500	540	9,268,200	566	9,805,700
1995	41	856,700	676	12,748,600	717	13,605,300
1996	23	359,900	594	8,627,600	617	8,987,500
1997	38	554,550	1,194	20,376,250	1,232	20,930,800
1998	32	582,350	916	16,741,000	948	17,323,350
1999	18	296,000	586	10,252,800	604	10,548,800
2000	9	104,500	746	13,163,500	755	13,268,000
2001	10	105,000	1,806	28,822,600	1,816	28,927,600
2002	0	0	1,910	35,031,300	1,910	35,031,300
Total	**1970**	**28,750,927**	**15,269**	**266,986,990**	**17,239**	**295,737,917**

* Offline and Open = Closed and open accounts.

Source: The Housing Bank, June 2003.

The Housing Bank

This was established by Amiri Decree in March 1979 as a joint stock company with an authorised capital of BD40 million (US$106.1 million), of which BD15 million (US$39.8 million) was fully paid up and subscribed to in its entirety by the Ministry of Housing (now the Ministry of Housing and Agriculture), under whose direction the Bank operates.

Exhibit 4.13: The Housing Bank - houses open, 1980-2002

Year	*Closed**	*Open**	*Total*
1980	235	623	858
1981	197	723	920
1982	256	1,060	1,316
1983	337	1,202	1,539
1984	76	95	171
1985	347	1,245	1,592
1986	244	689	933
1987	336	819	1,155
1988	172	471	643
1989	380	1,127	1,507
1990	196	600	796
1991	46	196	242
1992	278	946	1,224
1993	244	121	365
1994	296	119	415
1995	124	456	580
1996	36	144	180
1997	20	120	140
1998	75	18	93
1999	21	12	33
2000	77	530	607
2001	127	190	317
2002	0	1,041	1,041
Total	**4,120**	**12,547**	**16,667**

*Closed and Open = past and existing accounts.

Source: The Housing Bank, June 2003.

The prime responsibility of The Housing Bank is to develop the construction industry in Bahrain, in line with government policy to provide housing for the country's growing population. To this end the Bank offers loans to Bahraini citizens to allow them to build, purchase, expand or repair houses for their own occupation.

All such loans are provided at below-market interest rates to enable low-income families to participate.

Bank of Bahrain and Kuwait

Additionally the Bank:

- acquires land for the purpose of developing residential and commercial property;
- encourages the construction of factories to produce construction-related materials; and
- undertakes banking operations integral to the achievement of its objectives.

Some years after its formation, the Bank also became involved in the provision of finance for land reclamation for both commercial and residential developments and in the construction of areas for light industries.

ABC dealing room

In its first year of operation the Bank financed projects worth BD5.3 million (US$14.1 million) but did not extend any loans. By the end of 2002 the value of loans that had been extended since inception totalled BD295.7 million (US$788.5 million), comprising 16,667 houses and 17,239 loans.

In undertaking its activities The Housing Bank has always sought to operate in an open and transparent manner according to usual commercial parameters, despite being wholly owned by the government. Its books are fully audited by independent accountants and auditors each year, with the investment company complying fully with International Accounting Standards (IAS), specifically IAS40.

Overall, the Bank's activities have been wholly integral to the enhancement of the citizens of Bahrain, whilst also ensuring the provision of increased numbers of employment opportunities for the indigenous population and the stimulation of growth in the country's construction sector.

5 International banking

Offshore banking units (OBUs)

Following early growth in local commercial banks, the BMA recognised in 1973 that the local banking community at that time had limited capacity for dealing with the large amounts of money then circulating. With this and the country's desire for economic diversification in mind the BMA realised the country could become the major international financial centre for the whole Middle East, and started to draw up plans to this end. From the outset the BMA took what was to be a landmark decision to allow offshore banking units (OBUs) to operate out of Bahrain as a channel for investing the region's surplus liquidity, whilst recognising that to attract foreign banks to the market an attractive package would need to be provided to prospective participants.

So, a package of incentives was devised for OBUs that included exemption from maintaining reserves with the BMA and from observing the liquidity requirements laid down for the country's domestic banks, although they are subject to separate such requirements. Crucially, Bahrain was able to offer potential participants political stability and a relatively free economic system; freedom from exchange and trade controls; a tax efficient environment; adequate infrastructure, including world-class telecommunications; excellent airline connections to worldwide destinations; all utilities; readily available office and commercial accommodation; and a comfortable environment in which to live and work. Given such incentives and the highly conducive environment, allied to the increasing wealth of the Gulf States and their peoples at this

Citibank

time, the prospects for establishing banks and financial institutions in Bahrain were encouraging and the response was to prove enthusiastic.

When the BMA initiated the idea of internationalising the Bahraini banking sector in 1973, there were 11 commercial banks in operation with total assets of US$498.9 million (BD188.1 million). The first OBUs to start operation – Citibank and Algemene Bank – did so in 1975 but by the end of 1977 30 OBUs had been formed and their assets had already increased from US$1.7 billion (BD636 million) in 1975 to US$6.2 billion (BD2.3 billion). By 1984 the number of OBUs had reached 76 but, in the light of international developments and the growing trend towards the consolidation of banking groups, the number had fallen to 48 by 2002. At that time the total assets of the banking sector, now comprising 111 commercial, offshore, Islamic and investment banks, amounted to US$74.0 billion (BD27.8 billion), of which total OBUs accounted for US$58.8 billion (BD22.1 billion), about 11 times Bahrain's GDP. Long before this time, in the early 1980s, however, Bahrain had attained the desired mantle of the region's major international centre for banking and finance.

Under the terms of their establishment in Bahrain, OBUs were expected to establish a fully staffed operational base in the country, which had to be a branch of the parent company (although now they can be locally incorporated) and which had to conform with detailed reporting requirements to the BMA, including the monthly provision of statistics, the quarterly provision of prudential data and the annual presentation of an audited balance sheet and profit and loss accounts. In working from Bahrain, the OBUs were allowed to handle only non-resident and non-Bahraini dinar business, although a provision exists whereby they may invest in development projects in the country that have been approved by the BMA, and they can also deal with other banks, the government and state-owned enterprises. There are no legal reserve requirements but an annual fee is payable to the BMA.

Whilst encouraging international banks to come to Bahrain the BMA continued to remain selective, only licensing those banks deemed of high international standing, and from as wide a geographical spread as possible. The BMA has proved most successful in this regard with numerous well-known names from across the globe maintaining a presence in Bahrain.

The minimum paid-in capital of an OBU, as for all banks, must be US$20 million (BD7.54 million), but appropriate levels are agreed with the Agency as considered suitable on a case-by-case basis. Such offshore banks must, however, maintain an adequate level of capital measured on a risk-weighted basis according to Basel Committee recommendations. In practice, the BMA sets a minimum risk–asset ratio of 12 per cent for all banks, which is 50 per cent higher than the Basel minimum recommended level of 8 per cent, and a requirement that deposit liabilities do not exceed a multiple of 20 times capital and reserves. Also on a case-by-case basis, the BMA reserves the right to require the provision of endowment capital (in the case of branches) and/or a letter of guarantee from the offshore bank's parent organisation and imposes an exposure limit on any single customer of not more than 15 per cent of a bank's total capital base.

HSBC Bank

Liquidity requirements are imposed subject to the nature of the banks' core business. However, it is anticipated that primary liquid assets, defined as placements with less than one month to maturity, and any other short-term marketable investments, should not make up less than 25 per cent of total deposit liabilities.

Like most international financial centres, Bahrain has developed largely as an interbank market, a regional and international wholesale money centre. The precise type of business transacted varies from institution to institution, with some OBUs being solely marketing and administration centres for the Middle East, whilst others provide a broadly based wholesale banking service to their clients, not only within the Gulf but also worldwide, or are simply fund-gathering centres for their head offices. Certain others have come to Bahrain in support of their large domestic and multinational customers' activities in the Gulf region. Some Arab banks also opened OBUs in Bahrain, as a way of establishing an international presence, and yet others were founded in the country. Amongst the latter were Gulf International Bank, established in 1975 by the governments of the GCC states through Gulf Investment Company, and Arab Banking Corporation, formed in 1980 by the Abu Dhabi and Kuwait Investment Authorities and the Government of Libya and which is today one of the largest banks in terms of total assets in the Middle East.

In addition to conventional OBUs, the BMA has sought assiduously to encourage the development of Bahrain as an Islamic financial centre, in which it has been highly successful, and has therefore encouraged the establishment of OBUs operating according to *Shari'a* principles. Such banks are expected to comply with regulations similar to those applicable to their conventional counterparties, the guidelines for which are enshrined in a comprehensive set of prudential regulations for Islamic banks (see Chapter 6).

As mentioned, the primary activities of the OBUs since inception have been wholesale money market and interbank operations – indeed the OBUs can be credited with having developed the money market in Bahrain (see Chapter 7). This has involved the acceptance of deposits from and the making of loans to non-residents of Bahrain in foreign currencies; dealing in foreign exchange with non-residents; and undertaking money and foreign exchange dealings with authorised banks in Bahrain. Exhibits 5.1 to 5.4 show the level of foreign exchange activities of these banks. (See Appendix 2 for a list of all OBUs.)

Overall, the presence of OBUs has been beneficial to Bahrain in a number of ways. These have included a positive contribution to the country's balance of payments and in providing employment for Bahrainis, and within the financial environment, to the development of the local capital market by participating in a number of bond issues over the years and by developing a forward market in the Kingdom in regional currencies.

As at the end of May 2003 there were 51 OBUs licensed in Bahrain, of which three operated in accordance with Islamic principles, with total balance sheet footings as at end December 2002 of US$58.8 billion (see Exhibit 5.5). Of these funds, nearly 75 per cent were interbank deposits, thus clearly indicating the wholesale nature of the OBUs' activities. Exhibit 5.2 shows the geographical distribution of the sources of funding for the OBUs as at the end of 2002, and indicates that the majority emanated from within

Exhibit 5.1: OBUs - Geographical distribution of assets, 2001-02 (US$ million)

Period	*Bahrain*	*GCC*	*Other Arab countries*	*Americas*	*Western Europe*	*Asia*	*Other*	*Total*
2001	4,188.9	20,753.4	2,307.4	17,180.9	31,109.7	10,106.7	2,723.7	88,370.7
2002	3,968.6	16,677.0	2,001.3	12,423.7	18,514.0	4,662.1	569.1	58,815.8

Source: Bahrain Monetary Agency, *Quarterly Statistical Bulletin*, December 2002.

Exhibit 5.2: OBUs - Geographical distribution of liabilities, 2001-02 (US$ million)

Period	*Bahrain*	*GCC*	*Other Arab countries*	*Americas*	*Western Europe*	*Asia*	*Other*	*Total*
2001	5,557.0	24,091.4	5,881.7	8,783.4	29,292.0	14,401.8	363.4	88,370.7
2002	5,358.1	21,436.6	6,390.5	1,701.9	20,266.2	3,456.4	206.1	58,815.8

Source: Bahrain Monetary Agency, *Quarterly Statistical Bulletin*, December 2002.

Exhibit 5.3: OBUs - Classification of assets by major currencies, 2001-02 (US$ million)

Period	*BD*	*GCC*	*US$*	*GBP*	*Euro*	*DM*	*Yen*	*Other*	*Total*
2001	371.6	9,610.9	60,322.6	4,289.0	10,973.7	120.4	1,445.2	1,237.3	88,370.7
2002	347.0	6,727.3	43,350.7	1,489.7	5,086.0	40.3	758.3	1,016.5	58,815.8

Source: Bahrain Monetary Agency, *Quarterly Statistical Bulletin*, December 2002.

Exhibit 5.4: OBUs - Classification of liabilities by major currencies, 2001-02 (US$ million)

Period	*BD*	*GCC*	*US$*	*GBP*	*Euro*	*DM*	*Yen*	*Other*	*Total*
2001	312.7	10.059.9	61.221.2	3,825.6	9.949.1	763.3	1,247.6	991.3	88,370.7
2002	258.4	8,368.9	42,430.1	1,379.9	4,927.7	.9	628.7	821.2	58,815.8

Source: Bahrain Monetary Agency, *Quarterly Statistical Bulletin*, December 2002.

the Arab World excluding Bahrain (47 per cent) – largely from the GCC countries – and from Western Europe (34 per cent). Bahrain, Asia and the Americas, in diminishing order, were the other primary origins of funding. A not dissimilar picture emerges with fund utilisation (see Exhibit 5.1). Western Europe absorbed 31.5 per cent of the total and the Arab World (excluding Bahrain) 31.8 per cent. The Americas, Asia and Bahrain in declining order were the other areas of fund utilisation.

Exhibit 5.5: OBUs – consolidated balance sheet – assets, 1992-2002 (US$ million)

	Domestic assets					*Foreign assets*						
Year	*Banks**	*Private non-banks*	*General government*	*Other***	*Total*	*Banks*	*Non-banks*	*Securities*	*HO and affiliates*	*Other ***	*Total*	*Total assets*
1992	2,345.0	854.0	0	356.0	3,555.0	9,896.0	10,630.0	4,057.0	41,532.0	97.0	66,212.0	69,767.0
1993	2,526.0	807.0	0	458.0	3,791.0	8,415.0	16,187.0	4,568.0	27,216.0	22.0	56,408.0	60,199.0
1994	2,102.0	856.0	0	480.0	3,438.0	7,200.0	20,658.0	4,645.0	28,489.0	34.0	61,026.0	64,464.0
1995	3,033.0	750.0	0	503.0	4,286.0	8,783.0	11,736.0	5,173.0	34,208.0	64.0	59,964.0	64,250.0
1996	2,483.8	654.1	0.2	401.9	3,540.0	9,742.2	10,727.1	6,149.9	36,747.1	12.6	63,378.8	66,918.7
1997	2,429.0	779.7	0.2	577.3	3,786.2	11,565.6	13,373.3	7,076.9	36,199.8	51.6	68,267.2	72,053.4
1998	2,633.5	682.0	39.9	169.6	3,524.9	9,549.3	15,227.3	8,252.3	50,995.6	81.6	84,106.0	87,630.9
1999	2,964.6	635.6	64.6	156.4	3,821.2	11,283.0	14,501.0	10,216.1	48,235.4	99.6	84,335.1	88,156.3
2000	3,461.7	538.1	64.0	261.6	4,189.8	10,592.4	13,936.4	11,873.6	47,750.0	27.7	84,180.1	88,369.9
2001	3,298.6	529.2	100.4	261.6	4,189.8	10,592.4	13,936.4	11,873.6	47,750.0	27.7	84,180.1	88,369.9
2002	3,021.7	533.9	119.2	293.8	3,968.8	9,324.7	14,002.2	16,372.3	15,095.1	52.9	54,847.2	58,815.8

* Includes head offices and affiliates.
** Includes securities.

Source: BMA Quarterly Statistical Bulletin, December 2002.

Exhibit 5.6: OBUs – consolidated balance sheet – liabilities, 1992-2002 (US$ million)

	Domestic liabilities					*Foreign liabilities*						
Year	*Banks**	*Private non-banks*	*General government*	*Other***	*Total*	*Banks*	*Non-banks*	*Securities*	*HO and affiliates*	*Other ***	*Total*	*Total liabilities*
1992	3,198.0	704.0	639.0	866.0	5,407.0	10,781.0	14,564.0	-	37,114.0	1,901.0	64,360.0	69,767.0
1993	2,864.0	353.0	214.0	1,407.0	4,838.0	10,297.0	18,763.0	-	24,949.0	1,352.0	55,361.0	60,199.0
1994	2,566.0	432.0	403.0	8.0	3,409.0	10,536.0	23,705.0	-	25,100.0	1,714.0	61,055.0	64,464.0
1995	3,673.0	507.0	920.0	238.0	5,338.0	13,306.0	13,032.0	-	30,153.0	2,421.0	58,912.0	64,250.0
1996	2,747.2	633.1	985.3	426.1	4,791.8	13,660.2	14,211.8	-	28,904.6	5,350.5	62,127.0	66,918.7
1997	3,408.8	930.4	633.1	857.6	5,829.9	16,041.0	16,685.9	-	28,062.8	5,433.9	66,223.6	72,053.4
1998	3,717.4	1,074.4	337.3	318.5	5,447.5	17,049.1	21,143.7	357.6	40,249.8	3,383.1	82,183.3	87,630.8
1999	4,277.5	924.9	289.4	338.3	5,830.1	16,826.0	20,149.8	307.6	41,185.7	3,857.0	82,326.1	88,156.2
2000	4,307.5	636.0	323.3	385.8	5,652.6	19,789.4	20,616.7	590.1	42,097.3	4,290.1	87,383.6	93,036.2
2001	4,025.3	425.6	437.2	668.6	5,556.7	18,416.0	16,820.6	558.2	42,860.5	4,157.9	82,813.2	88,369.9
2002	3,560.7	447.1	352.3	998.0	5,358.1	20,289.5	12,507.6	1,107.5	15,408.2	4,144.9	53,457.7	58,815.8

* Includes head offices and affiliates.
** Includes capital and reserves.

Source: BMA Quarterly Statistical Bulletin, December 2002.

In currency terms, as at the end of 2002, the US dollar was by far the major transaction currency being the source of 72.1 per cent of all funds and 73.7 per cent of all fund utilisation (see Exhibits 5.3 and 5.4).

An area the OBUs are increasingly pursuing is project finance as the Gulf States have a wealth of infrastructural, developmental and downstream oil and gas projects in hand or under consideration. Historically, project finance activities have been handled to a substantial extent either by financial institutions outside the Gulf or by foreign banks and bankers operating in the region. As regional bankers become more proficient in handling such activities, so the BMA anticipates increased potential for encouraging the pursuit of project finance by locally incorporated institutions.

Investment banks

A third type of banking licence, after full commercial and offshore banking licences, was announced by the BMA in October 1977 and was designated an Investment Banking Licence. This licence was intended to allow financial institutions to participate in typical merchant or investment banking business with the primary aim of earning fees, whilst also fulfilling a role in fostering the capital market in Bahrain. The first such licence was issued late the same year to Bahrain Investment Bank.

A decision was taken from the beginning that, as with OBUs, to encourage the growth of investment banks all regulations governing them should be kept proportionate. Thus the regulations specify that the investment banks should have a minimum paid-in capital of US$10 million (BD3.77 million), or as otherwise agreed with the BMA, a minimum risk–asset ratio of 12 per cent and deposit liabilities not exceeding a multiple of 10 times capital and reserves. As to liquidity, liquid assets equal to 25 per cent of total deposit liabilities were deemed necessary. Furthermore, an investment bank must maintain a permanent fully staffed office in the country in order to undertake the range of activities envisaged at the outset by the BMA. These may include all forms of securities business, investment advice, capital raising and underwriting plus a limited amount of banking in the forms of loans and advances, but not overdrafts, and the taking of deposits from banks in Bahrain and outside and from non-banks outside Bahrain. These must be for a minimum of US$50,000 (BD18,850) and the funds cannot be held on current accounts.

Islamic investment banks are also very much encouraged, are licensed in a manner similar to conventional investment banks and number today just under half of all licensed investment banks. The major difference is the liquidity requirements, which are identical to those applicable to Islamic OBUs.

As to reporting requirements, a standardised monthly statistical report has to be returned to the BMA as does a quarterly prudential data statement and annual audited balance sheet and profit and loss accounts (in accordance with specifically defined criteria for Islamic institutions). An annual fee is payable to the BMA.

As with the previous two banking sectors, the number of investment banks licensed at any one time has fluctuated over the years but as at the end of May 2003 there were 36 with total assets of US$4,484.8 million (BD1,681.8 million).

Geographical distribution of the assets and liabilities of the investment banks was not markedly dissimilar to those of the OBUs, with most deposits, as at the end of 2002, emanating from within the GCC, including Bahrain, and totalling US$3.03 billion or 67.6 per cent of the total (see Exhibit 5.8). Most placements were in the Americas or Western Europe and absorbed 62 per cent of the total or US$2.79 billion (see Exhibit 5.7). The major transaction currency was the US dollar, which provided 92 per cent of all deposits and absorbed 87 per cent of all placements (see Exhibits 5.9 and 5.10).

The perception is that the investment banks will have a prominent role in years to come in further developing conventional and Islamic private banking and asset management from their bases in Bahrain, where private banking assets as at end 2002 amounted to US$22 billion. Estimates suggest there to be private wealth of around US$1.3 trillion in the Middle East, 80 per cent of which is in the GCC, much of which is today handled outside the region. Given that Bahrain offers full client confidentiality, free capital flow, tax efficiency, an innovative financial environment and a concentration of both conventional and Islamic financial institutions (IFIs), indications are the country is exceptionally well placed to enhance its position as a centre for private banking and asset management.

Representative offices

The BMA realised that a number of banks and financial services companies were interested in maintaining a presence in Bahrain, but that they did not wish to participate

Exhibit 5.7: Investment banks - Geographical distribution of assets, 2001-02 (US$ million)

Period	*Bahrain*	*GCC*	*Other Arab countries*	*Americas*	*Western Europe*	*Asia*	*Other*	*Total*
2001	626.4	633.0	146.8	1,367.6	1,152.1	98.9	9.1	4,033.9
2002	712.8	724.6	140.8	1,503.9	1,286.7	106.9	9.1	4,484.8

Source: Bahrain Monetary Agency, *Quarterly Statistical Bulletin*, December 2002.

Exhibit 5.8: Investment banks - Geographical distribution of liabilities, 2001-02 (US$ million)

Period	*Bahrain*	*GCC*	*Other Arab countries*	*Americas*	*Western Europe*	*Asia*	*Other*	*Total*
2001	1,191.2	1,797.5	174.7	389.6	426.3	31.6	23.0	4,033.9
2002	1,329.1	1,702.8	208.5	786.2	388.5	17.1	52.6	4,484.8

Source: Bahrain Monetary Agency, *Quarterly Statistical Bulletin*, December 2002.

Exhibit 5.9: Investment banks - Classification of assets by major currencies, 2001-02 (US$ million)

Period	*BD*	*GCC*	*US$*	*GBP*	*Euro*	*DM*	*Yen*	*Other*	*Total*
2001	146.4	275.3	3,509.6	19.0	24.7	0.0	18.5	40.4	4,033.9
2002	155.6	256.0	3,909.8	50.3	60.4	0.0	8.4	44.3	4,484.8

Source: Bahrain Monetary Agency, *Quarterly Statistical Bulletin, December 2002.*

Exhibit 5.10: Investment banks - Classification of liabilities by major currencies, 2001-02 (US$ million)

Period	*BD*	*GCC*	*US$*	*GBP*	*Euro*	*DM*	*Yen*	*Other*	*Total*
2001	134.3	150.0	3,636.2	30.0	54.4	0.0	13.4	15.6	4,033.9
2002	138.6	112.4	4,105.5	68.8	35.1	0.0	9.9	14.5	4,484.8

Source: Bahrain Monetary Agency, *Quarterly Statistical Bulletin*, December 2002.

directly in banking or other financial business in or from Bahrain – and thus did not require an offshore banking or investment banking licence. So a decision was taken in 1976 to license representative offices.

The activities of such offices are confined to the general promotion of products and services available from their head offices, the provision of general assistance to clients within the Middle East and to the gathering of economic, financial and commercial

Exhibit 5.11: Investment banks - consolidated balance sheet - assets, 1992-2002 (US$ million)

	Domestic assets					*Foreign assets*						
Year	*Banks***	*Private non-banks*	*General government*	*Other****	*Total*	*Banks*	*Non-banks*	*Securities*	*HO and affiliates*	*Other ****	*Total*	*Total assets*
1992	143.0	265.0	0.5	173.0	581.5	687.8	140.0	434.1	241.0	200.0	1,702.9	2,284.4
1993	105.0	166.0	0.5	149.0	420.5	698.8	256.0	505.0	152.0	169.0	1,780.8	2,201.3
1994	50.3	125.4	0.4	206.2	382.4	600.1	271.3	537.1	252.0	177.8	1,838.3	2,220.6
1995	272.8	83.8	0.5	84.9	441.8	932.7	235.0	625.5	128.4	115.6	2,037.2	2,479.0
1996	64.3	85.4	0.5	80.5	230.7	842.9	353.5	543.8	487.2	84.6	2,312.0	2,542.7
1997	218.4	149.8	0.5	82.3	450.9	825.9	412.7	400.8	959.3	59.0	2,657.7	3,108.6
1998	317.1	115.4	1.3	76.8	510.6	299.6	372.9	618.1	1198.2	85.1	2,573.9	3,084.5
1999	437.1	158.0	1.1	85.5	681.7	289.3	456.7	593.7	1898.3	97.5	3,335.5	4,017.2
2000	338.9	150.0	1.0	88.7	578.6	206.2	301.9	687.5	1516.2	90.5	2,802.3	3,380.9
2001	328.1	197.9	4.3	96.1	626.4	244.4	439.1	663.9	1930.9	129.2	3,407.5	4,033.9
2002	375.9	221.6	11.8	103.5	712.8	253.7	470.3	556.92	380.3	110.8	3,772.0	4,484.8

** Includes head offices and affiliates.

*** Includes securities.

Source: BMA Quarterly Statistical Bulletin, December 2002.

Exhibit 5.12: Investment banks - consolidated balance sheet - liabilities, 1992-2002 (US$ million)

	Domestic liabilities					*Foreign liabilities*						
Year	*Banks***	*Private non-banks*	*General government*	*Other****	*Total*	*Banks*	*Non-banks*	*Securities*	*HO and affiliates*	*Other ****	*Total*	*Total liabilities*
1992	334.0	63.0	75.0	92.0	564.0	494.2	374.0	-	100.0	752.2	1,720.4	2,284.4
1993	488.0	52.0	61.0	123.0	724.0	282.7	329.0	-	73.0	792.7	1,477.3	2,201.3
1994	258.2	42.4	61.1	111.5	473.2	603.9	298.9	-	76.4	768.3	1,747.5	2,220.6
1995	483.0	41.3	62.2	167.5	754.0	585.2	361.3	-	58.3	720.2	1,725.1	2,479.0
1996	484.1	212.1	13.0	148.2	857.4	227.0	340.8	-	72.3	1045.3	1,685.3	2,542.7
1997	239.1	225.2	15.1	96.0	575.4	535.8	564.3	-	62.9	1370.2	2,533.2	3,108.6
1998	149.6	94.7	168.1	285.2	697.6	294.1	495.5	0.0	458.9	1138.3	2,386.9	3,084.5
1999	391.3	116.5	182.6	434.8	1125.2	489.9	829.6	0.0	473.4	1099.1	2,892.0	4,017.2
2000	396.5	114.7	170.1	361.1	1,042.4	519.1	462.8	0.0	286.2	1070.4	2,338.5	3,380.9
2001	317.5	183.9	169.6	520.2	1,191.2	796.3	477.7	0.0	380.9	1187.8	2,842.7	4,033.9
2002	414.8	190.7	173.2	550.4	1,329.1	747.4	672.7	0.0	318.2	1,417.4	3,155.7	4,484.8

** Includes head offices and affiliates.

*** Includes capital and reserves.

Source: BMA Quarterly Statistical Bulletin, December 2002.

Ministry of Finance and National Economy

information. Given no actual banking activity is to take place under the terms of these licences, there is no separate capital requirement and no need to file a report of their financial position to the BMA. Representative offices must, however, submit the names of their management personnel to the BMA and provide notification of any changes that take place and must pay an annual fee to the BMA.

As at the end of May 2003, 29 representative offices were licensed by the BMA, of which one represented an IFI. (A list of all representative offices appear in Appendix 4.)

A successful innovation

The development of Bahrain as an international banking centre has been an undoubted success providing as it does a diversity of financial services unsurpassed anywhere in the Middle East. Today, as banking sophistication increases across the region and domestic banks in neighbouring countries expand both in size and capability, so Bahrain remains well to the fore as the pre-eminent financial location.

Bahrain has always been the pioneer in the financial sector, being the location of both the first bank and the first international insurance agency in the Gulf. However, maintaining a leading position has necessitated not only foresight on the part of the government and the BMA but also entrepreneurial flair and innovation.

When the BMA was formed in the mid-1970s there were just a handful of banks in operation, important though they undoubtedly were. Today, there are almost 300 financial institutions, including companies in the insurance sector, licensed and in operation. Between them they offer a wide range of services, as diverse as could be found in any major financial centre in the world, to an equally diverse clientele from corporations to individuals throughout the GCC States and further afield. This level of success could not have been achieved without the introduction by the BMA of a strong regulatory and supervisory environment on a par with the very best internationally. The challenge of the future is to maintain that level of regulation and supervision whilst continuing to enhance the transparency of the market and thereby to ensure a growing interest in Bahrain as a financial destination of choice.

6 Islamic finance and banking

The growth of Islamic banking and finance in Bahrain

In the past 30 years Islamic finance has grown to become a major global industry. By the end of 2002 over 250 Islamic banks had been established in both Muslim countries and international financial markets. Assets managed in accordance with *Shari'a* law were estimated by the Institute of Islamic Banking and Insurance at that time to amount to some US$180 billion. More recent figures suggest assets exceed US$200 billion and are growing at a rate of 15 per cent a year.

The growth of Bahrain as an international centre for Islamic banking was in part inspired by the recommendation of the Organization of Islamic Conference (OIC) in 1978 that the Muslim world should have its own Islamic economic and financial systems. Bahrain was an obvious location in which to nurture and grow a centre of Islamic banking and finance as it was already becoming the leading financial hub in the Middle East and a prominent player in conventional global banking and finance. In addition, through the ongoing efforts of the BMA, it had created both the environment and the relevant legal framework.

The concept of Islamic banking and finance has resulted from the needs of those members of the Muslim community who wish to adhere closely to their faith in their performance of financial transactions. The first Islamic bank was established in 1963, in Egypt, but it was to be another 10 years, in the aftermath of the substantial rise in oil prices in 1973, before the Islamic banking sector was to make serious advances. Since that time, Islamic banking has seen an annual growth rate of about 10 per cent, although a major part of that growth occurred in the last decade of the twentieth century and the early years of the twenty-first century.

The history of Islamic banking in Bahrain can be traced back to 1979 when the Bahrain Islamic Bank first opened its doors. After a slow start, the more recent growth of the sector, as perceived by local bankers, and especially since 1998, has been rapid. Bahrain is now host to the largest concentration of Islamic financial institutions (IFIs) in the Middle East with a total, as at end May 2003, of 25, equating to two-thirds of all such institutions in the region. These 25 IFIs comprise four full commercial banks, three offshore banking units (OBUs), 16 investment banks, one representative office and one investment adviser/broker. There are also five Islamic financial support organisations.

In the light of the early success of Islamic banking and finance in Bahrain, a range of specialised Islamic products has been introduced, including leasing, syndicated loans and collective investment schemes, not only by those institutions specialising in Islamic activities but also local and international conventional banks, which have sought to establish dedicated Islamic subsidiaries or 'windows'; to cooperate with their Islamic counterparts in offering specialised products and services; or to participate together in financing arrangements.

Because of the support and attention given to Islamic banking by the BMA, allied to the ongoing development of legal, regulatory and supervisory frameworks to ensure proper direction and monitoring of its activities, the Islamic financial sector in Bahrain had grown in terms of assets to US$2.9 billion (BD1.09 billion) by the end of December 2003, a figure which itself indicates an increase of 116 per cent since 1998.

Overall the Islamic banking and finance sector is subject to very much the same general supervisory and prudential regulations as the conventional banks, including the Basel Committee capital adequacy requirements. Nevertheless, the BMA has devised comprehensive requirements for the Islamic sector, including the prudential regulations for Islamic banking which came into effect in January 2002 (see below).

The challenge posed by Islamic banking for the BMA has not been confined to ensuring the introduction of a comprehensive supervisory regime to protect all of the investors, customers and the local international financial centre. It has also included the need to ensure the widest possible development of these institutions to enable the provision of a broad range of services and the specific training needs required to ensure a high level of competence in all aspects of Islamic banking and finance amongst the

Exhibit 6.1: Consolidated balance sheet of the Islamic banks* - assets, 1998-December 2002 (US$ million)

	Domestic assets						Foreign assets						
End of period	*Cash*	*Invested with banks ** *	*Invested with private non-banks*	*Invested with govt*	*Others*	*Total*	*Invested with banks*	*Invested with private non-banks*	*Securities*	*HO and affiliates*	*Others*	*Total*	*Total assets*
1998	3.4	468.3	202.3	0.0	54.2	728.2	85.0	372.5	72.2	80.4	9.7	619.8	1,348.0
1999	5.1	598.0	242.4	0.0	55.5	901.0	110.4	446.7	85.1	120.0	14.0	776.2	1,677.2
2000	4.2	713.1	285.3	0.0	69.2	1,071.8	186.8	370.0	88.3	184.1	16.5	845.7	1,917.5
2001	4.3	733.9	333.9	21.5	67.9	1,161.5	172.1	489.3	94.5	529.9	10.8	1,296.6	2,458.1
2002	7.2	774.1	438.9	51.7	87.1	1,359.0	159.4	667.2	97.9	613.2	15.1	1,552.8	2,911.8

* FCBs, OBUs and investment banks. Includes unrestricted investment accounts.
** Includes head offices and affiliates.

Source: Bahrain Monetary Agency, *Quarterly Statistical Bulletin,* December 2002.

Exhibit 6.2: Consolidated balance sheet of the Islamic banks* - liabilities 1998–December 2002 (US$ million)

	Domestic liabilities						Foreign liabilities						
End of period	*Banks ** *	*Private non-banks*	*General govt*	*Capital and reserves*	*Other*	*Total*	*Banks*	*Non-banks*	*HO and affiliates*	*Capital and reserves*	*Other*	*Total*	*Total liabilities*
1998	68.7	472.0	20.6	210.6	17.2	789.1	69.9	138.1	44.4	306.5	0.0	558.9	1.348.0
1999	183.9	516.3	20.6	352.5	15.7	1,089.0	61.3	102.9	87.0	334.9	2.1	588.2	1,677.2
2000	140.9	576.9	33.2	281.4	38.5	1,070.9	72.7	124.5	122.9	525.4	1.1	846.6	1,917.5
2001	117.1	654.4	18.4	403.9	22.8	1,216.6	311.4	173.0	223.2	530.9	3.0	1,241.5	2,458.1
2002	258.2	793.3	18.1	536.2	28.5	1,634.3	367.5	177.8	162.1	555.8	14.3	1,277.5	2,911.8

* FCBs, OBUs and investment banks. Includes unrestricted investment accounts.
** Includes head offices and affiliates.

Source: Bahrain Monetary Agency, *Quarterly Statistical Bulletin,* December 2002.

management and employees working in licensed operations in and from Bahrain. This the BMA has succeeded in attaining with substantial support from the Bahrain Institute of Banking and Finance (BIBF), which initiated courses specially designed for Islamic bankers.

The figures shown in Exhibit 6.1 and 6.2 are for all types of Islamic banks operating out of Bahrain and show clearly the steady growth experienced over the years they cover.

Offshore Islamic banks and Islamic financial institutions (IFIs)

Although the first Islamic bank in Bahrain was established in 1979, the growth over the ensuing 15 years was only modest. By the beginning of 1994 there were still only five Islamic investment banks and one Islamic OBU. However, following the Gulf War in 1990–91 oil prices rose, as did revenues, and the demand for Islamic banking services increased markedly. Between 1994 and the end of March 2002 nine Islamic investment banks, two Islamic OBUs and one of each representative office and investment broker operating according to Islamic principles were established.

These offshore Islamic banks, as with their onshore relatives, would normally be of one of two types – those which co-mingle the funds of the investment account holders with those of the bank and invest both funds together, such that the resulting investments are shared between the investors and the bank according to their share in the capital, and those which keep investors' funds separate from those of the bank and the bank prepares a quite separate income statement and balance sheet from those of each fund. As will be seen, such differences compared with conventional banks have a marked impact on the regulation and supervision of IFIs.

The main forms of financing used by these institutions are:

- *Murabaha:* This involves the purchase by a bank of goods on behalf of a client who agrees to buy the goods at a later date or dates at a higher price, thus generating a profit for the bank between the two prices. This is the most popular form of transaction for Islamic banks and makes up a significant percentage of all Islamic bank assets in Bahrain. A majority of the assets of Islamic collective investment schemes are also mainly *murabaha* instruments.
- *Musharaka:* This is the sharing in the capital of a project, be it in the capital of an investment or joint venture or in a short-term financing. There are two types of such financing – constant *musharaka*, where the partners' shares in the capital remain unchanged for its duration, and declining *musharaka*, where one partner sells his share by installments to the other partner.
- *Mudaraba:* This is a transaction between a bank and its client whereby the former provides funds to the latter for a defined investment stipulated at the outset.

Other forms of financing include *ijarah*, or leasing; *salam*, the purchase or sale of a commodity for deferred delivery in exchange for immediate payment; and *istisna'a*,

Islamic architecture at Beit Al Qur'an

whereby a purchaser asks the seller to manufacture a specifically defined product using the seller's raw materials at a given price – in effect similar to *salam* but with the payment being made over time and not at the outset.

The regulation and supervision of IFIs

From the outset it must be recognised that the primary regulation of all IFIs arises from the need for their compliance with *Shari'a* law, which strictly forbids what is called in Arabic *riba*, or interest. To overcome this, IFIs use a number of means of financing to derive returns for their investors, not depositors, based on transactions associated in one form or another with tangible assets. The returns must not in any way be guaranteed if they are to be in full concordance with the tenets of Islamic jurisprudence.

To ensure the ongoing compliance of any IFI it must have a *Shari'a* supervisory board (SSB) appointed by the shareholders and whose members are drawn from the ranks of respected, knowledgeable Islamic scholars. Such a SSB must be quite independent of a bank's main board of directors, although it may operate from within the bank it is advising. To ensure credibility and satisfaction of their customers' ethical expectations, many Islamic banks do maintain their SSB in-house and all new products and services are passed by it for approval before being introduced.

In referring to *Shari'a* principles notice must also be taken of the references made earlier to 'investors' rather than 'depositors' and to 'restricted and unrestricted investment accounts' as these are important differences when compared with conventional banks when contemplating the regulation and supervision of IFIs.

As indicated, there has been considerable growth in Islamic banking and finance in Bahrain and the BMA, in recognising the importance of this sector, has sought also to ensure its own full regulation and supervision without contradicting *Shari'a* law in any way, thereby enhancing the confidence of those operating in the sector and their investors. With this in mind the BMA has developed the 'Prudential Information and Regulatory Framework for Islamic Banks' (PIRI). The ultimate objective of PIRI is to provide a regulatory framework including a comprehensive reporting system to enable regular monitoring of banks' operations. Such monitoring assesses capital adequacy, asset quality, management of investment accounts, earnings quality and liquidity management, terminology very much the same as that applicable to conventional banks but sometimes different in structure and content. In introducing PIRI, the BMA sought not only to supervise and control Islamic banks but also to ensure the banks themselves had effective criteria to monitor their own activities and operations on a regular basis, so as to enhance their performance.

A further move by the BMA has been pursuit of what it describes as its 'Numu' (growth) strategy, a part of which is its own Islamic Banking and Takaful Task Force, which is proving to be an effective forum for the BMA, bankers and the private sector for strengthening the Islamic banking system.

The Accounting and Auditing Organization for Islamic Financial Institutions (AAOIFI)

To increase transparency and accountability within IFIs, AAOIFI was founded in 1990 and first registered in Bahrain in 1991 as an international, autonomous, non-profit-making body, with the task of setting acceptable standards for accounting, auditing, governance and transparency for IFIs, which would be applicable worldwide. As a result of AAOIFI's early activities, which were undertaken in close cooperation with bodies such as the International Accounting Standards Board (IASB), a set of guidelines on reporting and accounting practices has been drawn up introducing for the first time a measure of standardisation for Islamic banking. The BMA was the first central bank to approve the guidelines and to establish interrelated regulations for the Bahrain market, with Sudan and Jordan subsequently making all the standards and statements mandatory for their domestic financial institutions and several other countries, including Qatar and Saudi Arabia, using them as a basis for their regulatory standards.

AAOIFI's objectives are to:

- develop accounting, auditing, governance and ethical thought relating to the activities of IFIs, taking into consideration the international standards and practices that comply with *Shari'a* principles;
- disseminate the accounting, auditing, governance and ethical thought relating to the activities of IFIs and its application through training seminars, publication of periodical newsletters, preparation of reports, research and through other means;
- harmonise the accounting policies and procedures adopted by IFIs through the preparation and issuance of accounting standards and the interpretations of the same to the said institutions;
- improve the quality and uniformity of auditing and governance practices relating to IFIs through the preparation and issuance of auditing and governance standards and the interpretation of the same to the said institutions;
- promote good ethical practices relating to IFIs through the preparation and issuance of codes of ethics to these institutions;
- achieve conformity or similarity – to the extent possible – in concepts and applications among the *Shari'a* supervisory boards of IFIs to avoid contradiction and inconsistency between the *fatwa* and their applications by these institutions, with a view to activate the role of the SSBs of IFIs and central banks

Bahrain Islamic Bank

through the preparation, issuance and interpretations of *Shari'a* standards and *Shari'a* rules for investment, financing and insurance; and

- approach the concerned regulatory bodies, IFIs, other financial institutions that offer Islamic financial services, and accounting and auditing firms to implement the standards, as well as the statements and guidelines published by AAOIFI.

Following adoption by the BMA of AAOIFI's recommendations all IFIs operating in and from Bahrain must now comply with its requirements which, over time, are expected to be adopted far more widely, as they ensure compatibility between financial institutions, thus simplifying the work of entities such as the International Islamic Rating Agency (IIRA) and enhancing transparency and the level of disclosure.

Capital adequacy

All Islamic banks are expected to maintain an adequate level of capital, which the BMA has set at a figure of 12 per cent, as for conventional banks. Furthermore, and to cater to the fiduciary and displaced commercial risk of Islamic banks, the further recommendations of AAOIFI's 'Statement on the Purpose and Calculation of the Capital Adequacy Ratio for Islamic Banks' have also been adopted by the BMA. These recommendations make clear that investment accounts are not liabilities but are used to finance assets managed by a bank whilst at the same time a bank might need to utilise its own assets to absorb some of the risks of the assets under management, known as displaced commercial risk. It is thus the case that the BMA requires 50 per cent of the risk-weighted assets of the profit-sharing investment accounts to be included in the denominator of the capital adequacy ratio.

Asset quality

As with their conventional colleagues, Islamic banks must ensure they maintain assets of a sound quality and are thus expected to have policies and procedures in place to ensure the timely identification of any impairment and to have made adequate provisioning to reflect just such a situation. In this regard, the BMA expects banks to conform fully with the provisions relating to '*Mudaraba* Contracts – Minimum Terms and Conditions'. These state, amongst other things, that a comprehensive contract document be drawn up specifying the segregation, or otherwise, of the contract assets from the bank's assets and from the claims of the bank's own creditors. It should be stated also whether the assets of one *mudaraba* contract are to be commingled with the assets of other contracts.

In addition, the BMA has defined criteria for monitoring and control by all banks of large exposures. According to these criteria, notification must be made to the Agency where exposure to a counterparty will be equal to or exceed 10 per cent of the eligible capital base. Should the potential exposure be likely to exceed 15 per cent, the BMA must be given prior notification and must grant permission in advance.

Management of investment accounts

Management is charged with ensuring adequate policies and procedures are in place to safeguard the interests of both shareholders and profit-sharing investment account holders. Monitoring of compliance is carried out by the BMA through the medium of the returns completed under AAOIFI's Financial Accounting Standard (FAS) 11, which covers the provisions and reserves measurement and disclosure for Islamic banks. In particular, such returns necessitate full disclosure of a bank's profit equalisation and investment risk reserve. Definition is also required by the BMA from Islamic banks of the policies in place to safeguard profit-sharing investment account holders. The policy statement should include information on the basis for profit allocation and for making provisions and reserves; details of who the banks revert to in case of write-back or recovery; and the bank's policy on priority of investment and investment of current accounts. Furthermore, the banks are not permitted to transfer funds between restricted investment accounts and corporate books, carrying self-financed assets and those financed by unrestricted investment accounts, without the prior approval of the BMA.

Earnings quality

The BMA recognises a high level of earnings quality is essential to the long-term growth of any financial institution, be it Islamic or conventional, and therefore requires disclosure of banks' earnings, based on the amounts received with a breakdown of the ageing of the amounts receivable. A further breakdown of earnings is required, such as the earnings from the 10 largest customers, related parties and geographical spread. Such disclosure is intended to ensure the quality of earnings of the banks, thereby seeking to ensure their long-term growth.

Liquidity

Many transactions in Islamic banking are long term, whilst frequently the financing source is only short term. There is the potential, therefore, for Islamic banks to be exposed to a much higher liquidity risk than conventional banks, which makes the monitoring and control of liquidity one of the most critical responsibilities of an Islamic bank's management. This situation has been exacerbated in the past by the absence of interbank markets in which Islamic banks could participate, as they tend to be geared wholly to the concept of lending and borrowing with interest, therefore making them conceptually unacceptable. Hence the need for the introduction of the Liquidity Management Centre (LMC) in Bahrain, which provides asset-backed interbank liquidity for Islamic banks. Given the basic mismatch between long- and short-term liquidity, the BMA requires Islamic banks to undertake detailed monitoring of the situation, and has set mismatch limits for unrestricted investment accounts of 15 per cent for up to eight days and of 25 per cent for eight days to one month.

In addition, the BMA requires Islamic banks to monitor their liquidity mismatch position for both corporate books – that is self-financed assets and those financed by unrestricted investment accounts – and restricted investment accounts, and to agree a mismatch monitoring policy for the latter. However, on a consolidated basis, that is corporate books plus restricted investment accounts, the BMA has established a ceiling and timeframes identical to those for unrestricted investment accounts.

To encourage sound corporate governance, the BMA applies various requirements relating to IFIs' Boards of Directors and senior management. It also requires Islamic banks to comply with all accounting standards issued by AAOIFI, as well as the pronouncements issued by AAOIFI's *Shari'a* board, and to provide comprehensive information on their strategy, operations, management, personnel, risk management and internal audit, compliance and internal *Shari'a* review functions.

Furthermore, to ensure the development of the theory and practice of all aspects of Islamic banking and finance, the BMA also supports the Bahrain-based General Council for Islamic Banks and Financial Institutions (GCIBFI), to which such a role has been delegated (see below).

The development of Islamic *sukuk* (Islamic government bills and bonds)

Bahrain, through the BMA, has been the leader in the development of Islamic *sukuk* (literally, certificates), which are government bills and bonds acceptable to the Islamic investor. They are acceptable because they involve the leasing of tangible assets such as real estate. Under the scheme known as *sukuk al-ijarah* or leasing bonds, assets are held by the bondholders or by trustees who hold them on their behalf, who then lease them back to the original owner (currently the government), for a pre-determined period of time against which agreed payments are made on a six-monthly basis throughout the term of the lease. These payments provide the *sukuk* holders with their revenues but without interest being associated with the transaction.

By mid-2003 the Bahrain government had issued seven *sukuk al-ijara* totalling US$730 million, of which the issue of 27 May 2003 for US$250 million was the largest single offering of Bahrain Government Islamic bonds. The issue, which was arranged for the first time by the LMC in concord with the BMA, was the first bond issue to be made by the BMA through a market-maker and will provide a rental return, that is a yield to maturity, of 60 basis points over 6-month Libor, and will be paid semi-annually. Most issues are supported by unconditional guarantees issued by the Bahrain Government to buy the leased assets at maturity but this latest issue is also underwritten by eight major banks. *Sukuk al-ijara* have received an excellent reception from IFIs to the extent of being heavily over-subscribed. They have been proved Islamically acceptable due to their being asset-backed and suitable to be traded on stock exchanges, including on the Bahrain Stock Exchange, thus ensuring initial moves towards an Islamic capital market. As a result of their popularity, these Islamic financial instruments are also arousing interest among conventional banks.

The *sukuk* provide the opportunity to tap surplus liquidity in world markets in an Islamic manner, especially for IFIs, by serving their needs for medium and long-term investment opportunities. Ultimately, it is anticipated that *sukuk al-ijarah* will be traded rather than held to maturity as is the case now. This will open up a secondary market in Islamic instruments, thereby enhancing the role of the nascent International Islamic Financial Market (IIFM) (see below).

In addition to *sukuk al-ijarah*, the BMA has also taken the lead by issuing *sukuk al-salam*. Indeed, it was the first central bank in the world, in June 2001, to issue such an instrument. *Sukuk al-salam* are based on the issuing of a contract to commit to make a product for ultimate sale – in the case of Bahrain, aluminium. They are denominated in US dollars and have a short validity of just 91 days, making them an alternative to Treasury bills – although the *sukuk al-salam* may not be traded or discounted by the BMA due to the absence of a discounting mechanism unrelated to the payment of interest. This issue is, however, being addressed and may in part be solved following the development of the business of the LMC (see below).

By June 2003 25 issues of *sukuk al-salam* had been made – each for US$25 million – following detailed research by the BMA into their full compliance with *Shari'a* law and, subsequently, the issuance of a *fatwa*, a religious edict, by scholars at the Islamic Fiqh Academy in Jeddah following their agreement as to the acceptability of these instruments. The BMA's present programme of *sukuk al-salam* has been defined as lasting until 2004. Gulf-wide, estimates suggest that commodity-linked transactions have exceeded US$160 billion.

Islamic *sukuk* have been developed as an integral element of a move to establishing Islamic capital and money markets, including the IIFM, operating in accordance with Islamic jurisprudence, thereby enhancing the effective management of liquidity within the Islamic environment. To these ends, the *sukuk al-salam* are available for investment only by full commercial banks and all IFIs licensed by the BMA. In the event, there has been greater demand for *sukuks* from the conventional banks than from the Islamic institutions.

Success in developing and introducing *sukuks* has resulted in other GCC countries looking to Bahrain to manage their *sukuk* programmes, whilst both Brunei and Iran have sent delegations to examine potential for developing cooperation in this field.

The development of an Islamic financial infrastructure

Integral to the future development of Islamic banking and finance is a comprehensive infrastructure similar in concept to that applicable to conventional banks but without those elements proscribed by the *Shari'a*. To this end the BMA has been a leader in working with other central banks around the world and with other entities such as the Islamic Development Bank (IDB), AAOIFI and the GCIBFI in formulating and forming just such an infrastructure. Substantial progress has been made in this regard and, given Bahrain's role as the international financial centre of the Islamic world, the BMA has also ensured the presence of the underlying entities in Bahrain.

The International Islamic Rating Agency (IIRA)

As the operations of IFIs and the nature of Islamic financial instruments differ markedly from those of their conventional colleagues, it has proved difficult for international rating agencies to provide accurate or meaningful assessments of either. However, if the Islamic financial markets are to develop fully it is evident a dedicated rating agency is essential.

The idea for such an agency was initiated by the IDB and was subsequently established in Bahrain in October 2002 following close cooperation between a number of Islamic banks in Kuwait, Malaysia and Saudi Arabia, the international rating agency Capital Intelligence and the domestic rating agencies of Malaysia and Pakistan. The Agency's aim is to evaluate and rate Islamic banks and instruments and to make independent assessments similar to those of the conventional agencies, whilst giving full consideration to the appropriate *Shari'a* issues so critical to the Islamic sector, as well as the accounting and audit procedures laid down by AAOIFI. In short, the newly formed IIRA, which has been established as a profit-making company, will be a very specialised entity seeking to rate all IFIs and instruments worldwide to enhance the confidence of all participants in Islamic finance.

The objectives of the IIRA are to:

- carry out research, analysis, rating, evaluation and appraisal of the obligations, dues, commitments, shares, stocks and other securities issues;
- provide an independent assessment and opinion on the likelihood of future loss of a rated entity or a financial instrument within well-recognised analytical tools for determining the financial strength, fiduciary risk and credit-worthiness of the issuer;
- provide an independent assessment of compliance by the rated entity or financial instrument applying the principles of *Shari'a* law;
- disseminate, provide, sell, give, send, part with, dispose of and publish information, data and knowledge relating to rated entities or financial instruments;
- serve as an effective tool for introducing standards for greater disclosure and appropriate governance by way of presenting accounts and in assessing the governance systems of Islamic banks in accordance with AAOIFI;
- introduce a set of rating products and services, including *Shari'a* transparency, for both the financial instruments and their issuers;
- contribute to the promotion of international Islamic financial and capital markets and the instruments thereof.

In pursuing these objectives, the IIRA has recognised that to ensure its integrity is not undermined it must be wholly independent. This has been borne in mind when structuring the company and limitations have been imposed on individual shareholdings in the company.

Liquidity Management Centre (LMC)

For some time there had been a need for an intermediary agency to underwrite the trading of Islamic financial instruments and thereby to develop an interrelated financial market. In response to this need, the LMC was set up in February 2002 in Bahrain, with an initial paid-up capital of US$20 million and with the basic aim of creating an active secondary market for short-term *Shari'a*-compliant treasury instruments for Islamic banks and thereby enhanced liquidity of the Islamic banking market and additional investment opportunities for both financial institutions and private investors. The basic objectives of the LMC are: to enable IFIs to manage an asset/liability mismatch and to participate as both investors (providers of funds) and borrowers (providers of assets); to pool assets through the issuance of tradeable short-term asset-backed treasury instruments, *sukuks* in which IFIs can invest surplus liquidity; to provide short-term investment opportunities that have greater *Shari'a* credibility and are more competitively priced than commodity *murabaha* transactions presently undertaken in the market; to enable IFIs to assume term risk, securitise and liquidate such assets to improve the quality of their portfolios; and to seek to create secondary-market activity with designated market-makers where such instruments can be actively traded.

The banks funding the Centre at the outset included Bahrain Islamic Bank, Kuwait Finance House and Dubai Islamic Bank. Other IFIs are expected to join the LMC in due course.

The LMC, which commenced commercial operations in May 2003, is the first of its kind and is expected to provide a stimulus to the Islamic banking industry locally, regionally and internationally by addressing the critical need for liquidity management in line with *Shari'a* principles.

International Islamic Financial Market (IIFM)

The agreement to form the IIFM was reached in November 2001 with a board of directors representing monetary authorities in Bahrain, Brunei Darassalam, Indonesia, Malaysia and Sudan as well as the IDB. Based in Bahrain, the IIFM began operations in August 2002 as an Islamically acceptable global financial market with the primary purpose of providing a cooperative framework to ensure the continued growth of the Islamic financial market, based on *Shari'a* as a viable alternative to the conventional banking system. The venture's mission is to create and develop an international market for Islamic financial instruments by promoting and facilitating cross-border investment activity. In fulfilling this mission, the IIFM pursues roles that: promote the harmonisation and convergence of *Shari'a* interpretations in developing Islamic banking products and practices that are universally acceptable; encourage a large number of Islamic institutions to participate in the market by introducing a wide range of *Shari'a*-compliant products and the creation of an active secondary market thus providing liquidity to the instruments traded in the market.

The IIFM's future success is highly dependent on attracting a majority of the 250 plus Islamic banks and financial institutions worldwide; the creation of Islamic financial instruments; and the continued availability of adequate liquidity within the Islamic marketplace. To these ends, the IIFM seeks to encourage financial institutions, be they conventional or Islamic, to issue and list tradeable products compatible with the *Shari'a*.

The IIFM and the IIRA are expected to contribute considerably to the standardisation of all Islamic financial products and to make the whole Islamic financial sector transparent, competitive and viable as a potential provider of finance for economic development not only within the Muslim world but throughout the industrialised nations as well. In essence, the creation of specialised entities such as the IIFM, the LMC and the IIRA offers new alternatives and a wider choice to investors and users of funds worldwide and their foundation in Bahrain serves to underline the importance of the country as an international financial centre and the BMA as a highly respected regulatory and supervisory authority.

Within the context of Bahrain, the BMA would like to see the IIFM attract inward investment, increase liquidity of the Islamic financial sector and secure the country as the Gulf's principal banking centre.

The Islamic Financial Services Board (IFSB)

The formation of the IFSB arose from a recommendation made at a conference on 'Regulation in Islamic Banking' held in Bahrain in February 2000 and was registered in Malaysia in November 2002. At the time it was foreseen there was a need for a body made up of senior representatives of central banks within the Muslim world to formulate uniform standards of prudential supervision for Islamic products and firms. In the event, the founding members comprised the BMA, Bank Indonesia, Bank Markazi Jomhouri Islamic Iran, Central Bank of Kuwait, Bank Negara Malaysia, State Bank of Pakistan, the Saudi Arabian Monetary Agency, the Bank of Sudan and the IDB.

The following are the objectives of the IFSB:

- promote the prudent transparent and robust development of the Islamic financial services industry and markets through the promulgation of new standards or the adaptation of existing international standards consistent with the *Shari'a* mandate of the industry. These standards must be based on the recognition of the unique risks of Islamic financial products and practices;

- promote effective supervision and regulation of institutions offering Islamic financial products and to improve the basis for measurement, management and disclosure of risks. These regulations must take into account international standards of evaluation, income/loss recognition and disclosure, as developed for the industry;
- liaise and cooperate with relevant standard setters to facilitate international monetary and financial stability and the soundness of the financial systems of the member countries;
- enhance and coordinate initiatives to develop instruments and procedures for efficient portfolio and risk management standards;
- promote cooperation among member countries in developing the Islamic financial services industry; and
- facilitate the training and development of personnel in relevant areas such that they ensure effective oversight of the industry and related markets.

The organisational structure of the IFSB comprises a general assembly, composed of full and associate members and observers, an IFSB board, a technical committee and a secretariat.

General Council for Islamic Banks and Financial Institutions (GCIBFI)

The GCIBFI was founded during 2001 as a non-profit-making body, based in Bahrain, and with the broadly stated mission to 'work for the support of the Islamic banking industry with a view to promoting it through the dissemination of appropriate information and accurate data', thereby enhancing understanding of Islamic banking and finance on an international level.

The specific objectives of the GCIBFI have been defined as:

- informing the public regarding the concepts and rules governing Islamic banking and finance practices;
- enhancing cooperation between members of the council and other related institutions, such as regulatory bodies, in order to achieve common objectives;
- preparing and disseminating information and data pertinent to Islamic banking practices; and
- helping members face the challenges and problems in a collective manner in order to pave the way for success.

In fulfilment of these objectives, the GCIBFI prepares a range of publications; organises conferences, seminars and workshops addressing the same topics; and provides technical assistance and employee training programmes to its members. Integral to these activities is the establishment of a substantial database of the whole Islamic financial sector.

The future for *Shari'a*-compliant financial activities in Bahrain

For the sustainable growth of Islamic banking and finance based on strengthened investor and customer confidence, the BMA recognises there has to be a vision that embraces a regulatory framework, a sufficiency of support institutions, an environment of product innovation and the creation of facilities to generate and renew a pool of skilled talent. Much of what is needed is now in place, but the BMA retains its commitment to ensure the ultimate strengthening of the industry well into the future, to which end an Islamic banking and *takaful* (Islamic insurance) task force has been set up to undertake a strategic review of the sector and to develop initiatives to create new opportunities, so as to offer more sophisticated products.

Within the industry itself there is a strong recognition of the need for local Islamic banks to become increasingly international in outlook. Bahrain, as the worldwide hub for the sector with undoubted credibility, is an ideal location on which to build for the future as part of a global industry, especially given the availability of the many support organisations and activities, including high-quality training and education so integral to enhancing the standard of management and employees in the sector. Furthermore, Bahrain, given its progressive political and economic environments, is considered by many Islamic bankers as an ideal platform for expansion worldwide. As the populations and economies of countries across the Islamic world grow and become increasingly demanding, so the potential for Bahrain and its Islamic banking, finance and *takaful* sector would seem unbounded.

7
Non-banking financial institutions

Money brokers

Integral to Bahrain's strategy for establishing an international financial centre was the desire to develop a closely related money market. So the BMA decided to introduce licences for money brokers. The introduction of money brokers to Bahrain coincided with the vast flows of petrodollars being generated within the Gulf, as well as the decline of Lebanon as a Middle Eastern financial centre, and saw several banks move to Bahrain and create a money market.

When selecting the brokers, three criteria were considered paramount by the BMA: all participants had to be of the highest professional and international standing and repute; all had to be locally registered as domestic companies with a minimum of 51 per cent Bahraini ownership; and only that number of brokers would be allowed to operate according to the absorptive capacity of the market at any given time in the course of its growth.

In seeking the money brokers' involvement there was a clear desire to develop dealing not only in major international currencies but also to create a market in regional currencies. Bahrain has, in fact, become a major centre for Saudi riyal transactions. Equally as important was the wish to enhance the efficiency of the local and regional financial markets. To this end the BMA sought to encourage the banks, both onshore and offshore, to use the services of the money brokers, without any obligation for them so to do.

Money brokers in Bahrain operate in much the same way as elsewhere in the world. They facilitate transactions in financial instruments and foreign exchange, providing a specialised service to the banking community as intermediaries in the fields of spot and forward foreign exchange, borrowing and lending foreign currencies, deposits, certificates of deposit and, more recently, interest rate swaps and other derivatives.

Over time, a maximum of six money brokers, mainly affiliates of London firms but including one from Lebanon, established a presence in Bahrain, of which four remained licensed as at the end of the second quarter of 2003: Charles Fulton (Gulf) WLL; ICAP (Middle East) WLL; Marshalls (Bahrain) Limited; and Tullet and Tokyo (Bahrain) Company WLL.

In order to ensure good practice amongst the brokers, a code of conduct in regard to dealing practices was drawn up and issued in May 1985. Both brokers and banks are required to comply with the code's conditions which were reached after extensive discussions between the brokers, the BMA and the Banker's Society of Bahrain. Also integral to the standing of the market was the level of confidentiality which prevailed and the mutual trust generated between the BMA, the brokers and their customers. These were mainly regional financial institutions which were greatly helped at the time to trade on international markets by the knowledge of the brokers in Bahrain.

All brokerage charges are subject to agreements. Initially a scale of charges was set by the BMA but over time these were superceded by mutual agreement between all the parties involved, including the Banker's Society of Bahrain, and are revised as and when it is needed to ensure the international competitiveness of those operating in Bahrain. The charges as laid down are either flat or percentage rates depending on the underlying transaction, be it foreign exchange, deposits or derivatives, which rates may be subjected to volume discounts according to an equally well-defined scale. The discounting practices as laid down are deemed by the BMA to reflect sound business principles.

The BMA fully regulates and supervises all brokers through its financial institutions supervisory directorate and maintains a watching brief over their activities, including the issuance of circulars, on topics specific to the brokers, the making of inspections to ensure compliance and through analysis of the returns the brokers are required to make according to a predetermined schedule. In supervising the brokers the BMA's primary objectives are to maintain a stable and orderly market with well-capitalised licensees.

Chase Manhattan

Money changers

The primary functions of the money changers are the exchange of currencies and travellers' cheques for the general public, the issuance of foreign currency banks drafts and the telegraphic transfer of funds to worldwide destinations.

Money changing can be traced back in Bahrain to 1917, when the business known today as Bahrain Financing Co first established a presence four years before the first bank opened in the country. But that company and many of its competitors in later years were, in their earlier days, more involved in buying jewellery, smelting it and selling the gold bars on the London market. Some of these dealers also became involved in the borrowing and lending of money in the local marketplace.

The move into currency trading, the major facet of their business today, only began to take place in the early 1950s and even then was very limited in scope partly due to the economic hardship of the time and partly to Bahrain's membership of the Sterling Area. Then, as more expatriates arrived in Bahrain and had an increasing need to exchange currencies so a number of money changers started buying and selling foreign currencies and at least one began to buy currencies overseas to sell on to its customers in Bahrain. As this business grew and developed so the bigger money changers moved into the business of remittances around the world.

An important watershed for some money changers was the opening in 1986 of the King Fahd Causeway between Bahrain and Saudi Arabia resulting in a huge demand to exchange Saudi riyals and ultimately their repatriation to Saudi Arabia, which the money changers sought to do against the purchase of US dollars. Since then, and despite the marked growth in banking in the interim, the money changers have flourished. As at mid-2003, 17 money changers were operating in Bahrain (see Exhibit 7.1).

The money changers' prime clients are the numerous expatriates who live and work in Bahrain, especially but not exclusively those emanating from India, Pakistan, Bangladesh, the Philippines and Sri Lanka, often seeking to remit funds to their families at home, as well as the increasing number of tourists to the islands changing currencies and travellers' cheques. The attraction of the money changers to residents and tourists alike is their long opening hours, competitive exchange rates and the lower transaction costs incurred.

Money changing is a highly competitive business but one not without risk to both the money changers themselves and their customers. To be able to service the demands of clients on an on-going basis the money changers must, by definition, maintain not inconsiderable amounts of cash and, similar to the banks, must maintain accounts with financial institutions overseas on which to draw drafts or to which they remit funds. In order to minimise the risks, a decision was taken to officially regulate the money changers, in November 1984, when the Board of Directors of the BMA, under powers conferred by Amiri Decree No. 23 of 1973, introduced regulations governing their business and activities.

Initially a two-tier regulatory system was introduced with the holders of a Category A licence being permitted solely to buy and sell foreign currencies and travellers

Exhibit 7.1: Money changers operating in Bahrain, as at 30 June 2003

Name	*Number of branches*
Al-Manama Exchange	1
Al-Zamil Exchange Est.	1
AlYousuf Exchangers	2
Arexco WLL	1
Awal Exchange Co.	1
Bahrain Express Exchange	1
Bahrain Financing Co.	12
Bahrain India International Exchange Co.	5
Dalil Exchange	4
Delmon Exchange	1
Haji Yousuf AlAwadi Exchange Est.	1
Khalil Ibrahim AlFardan Exchange	1
Mandeel Exchange Co. WLL	2
National Finance & Exchange Co. WLL	2
Nonoo Exchange Co. WLL	2
World Exchange Centre WLL	1
Zenj Exchange Co. WLL	8

cheques, with Category B licence holders also being allowed to issue foreign currency drafts and to deal in precious metals. However, with effect from late December 1995, new regulations were issued combining the two categories in accordance with the previous Category B regulations, thereby broadening the scope of business of the former Category A licence holders.

The money changers are strictly regulated by the BMA to ensure their credibility and viability in the marketplace. Integral to the BMA's regulation of the money changers is the requirement, since 1 January 1996, that they should have a minimum capital of BD150,000 (US$397,878) and should post a guarantee with the Agency from a commercial bank in Bahrain for a minimum of BD50,000 (US$132,626), or such larger amount as may be requested from time to time. All money changers are expected by the BMA to produce annual audited accounts which must be prepared in accordance with International Accounting Standards (IAS) and are strictly controlled as to the distribution of profits; the taking and repaying of loans by owners and directors; and as to the level of their liabilities at any one time, which must not exceed a multiple of three times their combined capital and reserves.

Following implementation of the regulations, the practice of money changing is not permitted unless the practising company is duly licensed, although hotels and commercial establishments are permitted to exchange money and cash travellers' cheques, but solely for their own customers. Oversight of their activities is now undertaken by the financial institutions supervisory directorate.

Investment advisers and providers of other financial services

In November 1993 the BMA initiated new arrangements for the licensing, regulation and supervision of investment advisers and providers of other financial services thereby making them subject to regulatory and supervisory activities of the BMA. In introducing the licensing of providers of investment and financial advisory services the BMA was seeking at one and the same time to broaden the base of the financial services being offered in a properly regulated manner from Bahrain, whilst seeking to

Exhibit 7.2: Investment advisers/brokers

ASA Consultants
Capital Growth Management WLL
Corporate Finance International WLL
Erem Finance & Investment Consultants EC ©
Gulfinvest Bahrain WLL
H & A Investment Services Company WLL
Indogulf Financial Services WLL
Inter Alliance International Financial Services Limited
Islamic Finance Consultants EC*
Islamic Joint Venture Partners*
Pro-Capital Associates
Towry Law (Asia) HK Limited
United Investment Advisory WLL
Wealth Management Group WLL

* Operates according to Islamic principles.

ensure at least a measure of protection to investors and other users of the services against the possibility of unscrupulous practices.

The term 'investment' is intended to cover every aspect of dealing as principal or agent with any form of investment, be it shares, debentures, government and public securities, options or futures, whether arranging deals; managing, safekeeping or administering investments; providing investment advice; or providing any inter-related services duly authorised by the BMA. In practice, the activities covered by the regulation are confined to investment advice/consultancy, investment advice/brokerage and the provision of ancillary services to the financial sector.

As with other sectors regulated by the BMA, each of the three activity areas defined are subject to separate conditions and licensing criteria, outlined in Chapter 5, Offshore banking, but which includes the need to take out indemnity insurance against liability for any negligence that might occur.

At the end of June 2003 there were no licensed investment advisers/consultants but 14 investment advisers/brokers maintained a presence, two of which operate according to Islamic principles (see Exhibit 7.2). Four providers of ancillary services were also licensed at the same date – Bloomberg Tradebook Europe (Tradebook Europe); and The Benefit Company, which hosts the domestic and Gulf-wide ATM switch network; Gulf Clearing Company BSC ©; and Gulf Outsourcing Company WLL.

Leasing companies

Both conventional and Islamic leasing is an area which the BMA would like to see developed in the immediate future. As at mid-2003, there was only one leasing company registered in Bahrain – Overland Leasing Bank – although a number of Islamic banks and financial institutions undertake the leasing of ships, planes and equipment as part of their normal business. To ensure a properly regulated leasing environment, new regulations were recently issued.

The future for non-banking financial institutions in Bahrain

Integral to the BMA's plans for the future is the desire to encourage yet further financial support companies, which are so vital to the full development of Bahrain as an international financial centre. In so doing, controls will remain in place to ensure the level of growth of such non-banking entities is commensurate with the demands of the marketplace, whilst ensuring a competitive and free market.

8
Insurance

Introduction

From modest beginnings in 1950, the insurance industry in Bahrain has grown to become a prominent element within the country's financial services sector. In the 1950s and 1960s Bahrain was the Arabian Gulf's major trading centre, with its merchants having established commercial links with producers worldwide, a situation that continues to this day. As trade grew so there became an increasing need for insurance to protect the merchants' interests, which in turn led to the establishment not only of an increased number of local agents of international insurance companies but, over time, to the establishment of locally owned insurance companies.

In the 1970s, following the increase in world oil prices Bahrain became the financial centre for the region. Integral to this new-found role was the development of an offshore insurance industry, primarily serving Saudi Arabia, where the formation of domestic insurance companies was officially proscribed. The success of the policies designed to develop the insurance market is probably best seen in terms of the gross premiums written as the offshore industry accounted for some US$532 million (BD200.6 million) or 59 per cent of the total premiums written by Bahraini registered companies in 2000.

Until 2002 the development and growth of the industry had been based on regulation and supervision overseen by what is today the Ministry of Commerce, a role it has fulfilled effectively whilst also protecting the interests of policy holders. The mantle of regulation and supervision, however, passed to the BMA in August 2002, since when the Agency has moved quickly to examine the potential for introducing enhanced regulation of the sector.

Background

The first insurance agency in Bahrain, and within the Arabian Gulf, was established in May 1950 when the United Kingdom's Norwich Union Fire Insurance Society Ltd appointed Messrs Yusuf bin Ahmed Kanoo to be their 'sole and principal agents for the Bahrain Islands'. The insurance cover provided through this agency comprised a number of classes including fire, burglary, marine, life and motor insurance, with the latter being of special interest as all taxi drivers were required to have insurance cover for their vehicles.

However, though the taxi drivers recognised insurance to be essential, they found the level of premiums being charged to be onerous and thus elected to form a society financed by members' fees and mutually agreed periodic contributions. So successful was this initiative that, in February 1954, a wholly Bahraini-owned company was established called the Cooperative Compensation Society, whose specific activity was to insure drivers and vehicles against losses arising from accidents. This business was funded through the reserves the society held with local banks, the revenues arising from shareholdings in local cooperative projects and the fees paid by vehicle owners and drivers, whether members or not, as membership was open to all motorists, who subsequently were all expected to have at least third-party insurance. This society remained in operation until 1982 when its assets and liabilities were absorbed into the Vehicle Insurance Fund, which was itself taken over by the Gulf Union Insurance and Reinsurance Co. some years later.

The growth of the insurance sector

Insurance companies

In the 1970s, as the states surrounding the Arabian Gulf began to enjoy the unprecedented wealth arising from oil revenues, a number of new insurance companies were formed in Bahrain, among them being AlAhlia Insurance Co., Bahrain Insurance Company (which is now Bahrain National Insurance Co. following the merger with

Exhibit 8.1: Insurance companies operating in Bahrain, 2001

National companies
Bahrain National Insurance Co.
Bahrain National Life Insurance Co.
Bahrain Kuwait Insurance Co.
Al Ahlia Insurance Company
United Insurance Company
Takaful International Insurance Co.
Bahrain Norwich Insurance Co.
Gulf Union Insurance & Reinsurance Co.

Foreign companies
American Life Insurance Co.
New India Insurance Co.
Arabia Insurance Company
Iran Insurance Company
Northern Assurance Co.
AXA Insurance Company
Al-Nisr Insurance Co.
Royal Exchange Insurance Co.
Eagle Star International Life Ltd.

Source: Insurance Sector Activities in Bahrain, BMA Insurance Supervision Directorate, 2001.

National Insurance Co.) and Bahrain Kuwait Insurance Company. Today, there are eight national companies and nine branches of foreign insurance companies conducting direct insurance business in the Kingdom (see Exhibit 8.1). Of the national companies just one, Takaful International Insurance Co., operates according to Islamic criteria (*takaful*).

Premiums and claims

In 1950, its first year of operation in Bahrain, Norwich Union (according to its own records) collected premiums with a total value of just 22,529 Indian rupees, which would have approximated on the introduction of the Bahraini dinar to BD2,253

(US$5,976). In 2001, the gross premium income of the Bahrain insurance market had risen to BD58.6 million (US$156.3 million), with national companies booking 67.5 per cent of the total at BD39.6 million (US$105.6 million). Of the overall premium total BD30.9 million (US$82.4 million), approximately 53 per cent of the total, had been retained.

Claims in those early years were also modest, but by 2001 gross claims had reached BD31.1 million (US$82.9 million), of which net claims totalled BD20.4 million (US$54.4 million) (see Exhibit 8.2).

Sectorally, the major premium income was derived from two sources in 2001, motor and life insurance with premiums of BD23.5 million and BD13.0 million (US$62.7 million and US$34.7 million) respectively, or 62 per cent of the total gross premiums written. By far the largest claims that year were seen in the motor sector when BD18.4 million (US$49.1 million) was paid, 59 per cent of total gross claims (see Exhibit 8.3).

Exhibit 8.2: Premiums and claims of Bahrain insurance market (BD '000s)

	Gross premiums		*Retained premiums*		*Gross claims*		*Net claims*	
Companies	*2001*	*2000*	*2001*	*2000*	*2001*	*2000*	*2001*	*2000*
National insurance companies	39,603	33,421	20,209	17,312	21,168	20,045	11,835	10,352
Branches of foreign insurance companies	18,989	19,018	10,731	9,609	9,912	9,428	8,608	6,020
Total	**58,592**	**52,439**	**30,940**	**26,921**	**31,080**	**29,473**	**20,443**	**16,372**

Source: Insurance Sector Activities in Bahrain, BMA Insurance Supervision Directorate, 2001.

Exhibit 8.3: Premiums and claims of Bahrain insurance market, by class, 2000-01 (BD '000s)

	Gross premiums		*Retained premiums*		*Gross claims*		*Net claims*	
Sectors	*2001*	*2000*	*2001*	*2000*	*2001*	*2000*	*2001*	*2000*
Life	13,003	13,352	5,127	4,424	5,554	3,969	3,660	1,861
Fire	8,665	7,747	1,725	1,821	3,622	5,746	1,160	1,104
Marine	4,069	2,651	1,182	1,095	36	1,185	325	323
Motors	23,473	20,885	18,861	16,637	18,367	15,812	13,197	11,567
Miscellaneous	9,382	7,804	4,045	2,944	3,501	2,761	2,101	1,517
Total	**58,592**	**52,439**	**30,940**	**26,921**	**31,080**	**29,473**	**20,443**	**16,372**

Source: Insurance Sector Activities in Bahrain, BMA Insurance Supervision Directorate, 2001.

Offshore insurance companies

As the domestic market grew, so too did the number of offshore insurance companies. Following issuance of Ministerial Order No.25 of 1977, which encouraged their formation, the number of offshore insurance companies incorporated in Bahrain grew from just one in 1979, the Saudi International Insurance Company, to 83 by the end of 2001.

As is intended from the nature of their registration, these companies may operate solely outside Bahrain and the laws that are in place to prevent them from writing any direct insurance in the country are strictly enforced. Notwithstanding the fact their

Exhibit 8.4: Offshore insurance companies, 1996-2000 (US$ million)

Year	*Total assets*	*Gross premiums*
1996	591	385
1997	683	461
1998	816	493
1999	867	509
2000	928	532

Note: Local insurance market includes direct insurance companies, branches of foreign companies and Arab Insurance Group.

Source: Annual Insurance Report 2000 – Ministry of Commerce & Industry, Insurance Directorate.

Exhibit 8.5: Ten largest offshore insurance companies by total assets, 2000 (US$ '000s)

Trust International Insurance Company	97,755
Saudi Arabian Insurance Company Ltd	81,844
Islamic Insurance and Reinsurance	77,730
Life Insurance Company of India	56,691
Gulf Union Insurance and Projects Management Holdings	56,115
AlAlamiya Insurance Co. Ltd (ROTAL and Sun Alliance)	51,489
Arig Health & General Insurance Co.	42,840
Takaful Islamic Insurance Co. E.C.	40,404
U.C.A. Insurance Co.	34,631
Saudi National Insurance Co.	25,912
Total	**565,411**

Source: Annual Insurance Report 2000 – Ministry of Commerce & Industry, Insurance Directorate.

Exhibit 8.6: Ten largest offshore insurance companies by gross premiums, 2000 (US$ '000s)

Gulf Union Insurance and Projects Management Holdings	42,466
Saudi Arabian Insurance Company Ltd	37,402
U.C.A. Insurance Co.	37,070
AlAlamiya Insurance Co. Ltd (ROTAL and Sun Alliance)	34,316
Trust International Insurance Company	34,201
Saudi National Insurance Co.	28,375
Gulf Union Insurance & Risk Management	25,295
Islamic Insurance and Reinsurance	24,703
Arabian American Insurance Co. (Bahrain)	22,680
BUPA Middle East Limited	22,417
Total	**308,925**

Source: Annual Insurance Report 2000 - Ministry of Commerce & Industry, Insurance Directorate.

activities are undertaken entirely offshore, all such companies must also comply fully with all other laws and regulations that are applicable to the onshore companies registered and authorised to write direct insurance in Bahrain.

At the end of 2000 (the latest year for which detailed figures are available) the total assets of all offshore insurance companies amounted to US$928 million (BD349.9 million). This figure equated to 39 per cent of the total assets of the Bahraini insurance market (if the figures for the Arab Insurance Group are included). Gross premiums of the offshore companies at the end of the same year, however, accounted for a far higher proportion of gross premiums written at US$532 million (BD200.6 million) or 59 per cent of the market total (see Exhibit 8.4).

The 10 largest offshore insurance companies by total assets and gross premiums as at the end of 2000 are shown in Exhibits 8.5 and 8.6.

Reinsurance

Along with the development of the insurance sector in the Middle East, the rate of developmental progress in the region and rising premiums for cargo and hull insurance, which were having an adverse affect on the cost of imports to Arab countries, the demand rose for an increased level of reinsurance to be provided from within the Middle East. So, in 1980, Kuwait, Libya and the United Arab Emirates came together to form the Arab Insurance Group (ARIG), with an authorised capital of US$3 billion (BD1.1 billion). Subsequently, ARIG's reinsurance subsidiary was formed, ARIG Re, based in Bahrain. In 2000, ARIG Re was considered one of the largest reinsurance operations in the Middle East, having written BD49 million (US$130 million) in premiums over the course of that year.

The paid-up capital of ARIG is US$250 million (BD93.8 million) and the company's shares, are publicly quoted on the stock markets of Bahrain, Kuwait, Cairo and London (on the latter as GDRs). In the more recent past, however, the company has sought increasingly to transform itself into a financial services provider offering conventional non-life insurance products, life and medical insurance products (both direct and reinsurance) and financial and business services. As of June 2003 ARIG is one of three reinsurance companies in Bahrain, the others being Trust International Insurance and Labuan Re. The BMA is seeking to establish a *retakaful* company in due course.

Other insurance-related entities in Bahrain

As would be anticipated of a well-developed and regulated insurance market located at the heart of the Arabian Gulf, Bahrain has become an increasingly important location for all those entities so integral to the effective pursuit of the business of insurance. As of June 2003, there were a total of 154 insurance firms and brokers in Bahrain, including 24 registered insurance brokers; eight loss adjusters; seven insurance company representative offices, whose functions include liaison between international insurance companies and the research, collection and analysis of information on local and regional insurance markets and 14 providers of other insurance-related activities.

Furthermore, the Bahrain Insurance Association was established in 1993 to promote the interests of those companies actively involved in the direct insurance market, to further the business of insurance in the country and to enhance public awareness of insurance within the Kingdom of Bahrain.

In recognition of the importance placed on the proper performance of the insurance broking sector in Bahrain the 'Implementing Regulations Governing the Profession of Insurance Brokers' were amended in December 1998 to include the requirements that those people participating in the sector must pass specified examinations to become properly qualified and that those wishing to pursue the profession or to manage a broking company must have a number of years' experience of the technical aspects of the insurance business.

Insurance syndicates

As both insurance and reinsurance within the Gulf grew, the assessment of risk continued to be made by companies far away from the Middle East, with little or no knowledge of risk levels in the region. The need was therefore deemed necessary for a regional entity to make its own assessment of applicable risks and to apply rates commensurate with its assessment of the degree of hazard involved. Thus the Arab War Risk Insurance Syndicate (AWRIS) was formed in the 1980s, which today has a membership of more than 105 Arab insurance companies and is based in Bahrain. Also based in Bahrain is the Federation of Afro-Asian Oil and Energy Pool (FAIR OIL POOL), whose member base is in excess of 170 African and Asian insurance and reinsurance companies.

Captive insurance

Although Bahrain has sought to develop into an international insurance centre there has as yet been little activity in the captive insurance sector. Arguably some of the insurance companies established under exempt company regulations were captives as they were owned by individuals and privately owned businesses, particularly from Saudi Arabia, for their own purposes, but they were never regarded as true captive insurance companies. Legislation for such companies is therefore integral to ongoing discussions between the BMA, the local insurance community and the Bahrain Insurance Association, with the intention of its introduction at an opportune time as a basis for the development of the sector in the future.

Islamic insurance and reinsurance – *takaful* and *retakaful*

Insurance in accordance with the tenets of Islam has been slow to develop worldwide, including in Bahrain. Currently there is just one direct insurance company operating in

Bahrain according to the principles laid down in the Islamic *Shari'a*, that being Takaful International Co., although there are also a number of offshore companies in this sector. In 2001 this company had gross premium income of some BD1.89 million (US$5.04 million), or about 4.8 per cent of the total premiums written in Bahrain. The increasing popularity of *takaful* products is evidenced by the growth in premium income in 2002 to BD3.6 million (US$9.6 million), a growth figure of 92 per cent over the previous year, when medical and family *takaful* products were introduced, the latter being life insurance products based on Islamic principles.

The basic principles of protection under *takaful* are similar to conventional insurance based on the law of large numbers with both pricing their risks using experience ratings. However, *takaful* differs in the way it invests its funds, which must be in ethically acceptable investments approved under the principles of the Islamic *Shari'a*, that is, devoid of any usury and interest, which is known as *Riba*, and the structure must be such as to remove any semblance of gambling or exploitation from the underlying operations. The insurance fund is deemed to be owned by the policyholders based on cooperative principles, with profit sharing of the surplus so as to avoid over-pricing of the risk.

According to the London-based Institute for Islamic Banking and Insurance, in 2002 there were 46 *takaful* insurance companies worldwide (an increase of 18 from the previous year) writing *takaful* directly, and many fewer *retakaful* or reinsurance companies, resulting in the *takaful* companies having to reinsure through the conventional market – something Islamic scholars have permitted in the face of no viable alternative.

As Bahrain continues to be promoted as a centre for Islamic financial services and a comprehensive regulatory and supervisory environment is created, so a growth in the number of Islamic insurance and reinsurance companies in the country is anticipated. With regard to Islamic reinsurance, detailed consideration is being given to the formation of such a company in the foreseeable future.

Regulation and supervision

Although the business of insurance has been practised in Bahrain since the early 1950s, the sector remained largely self-regulatory until the promulgation of Legislative Decree No. 17 of 1987 with respect to 'Insurance Companies and Organisations' and its sup-

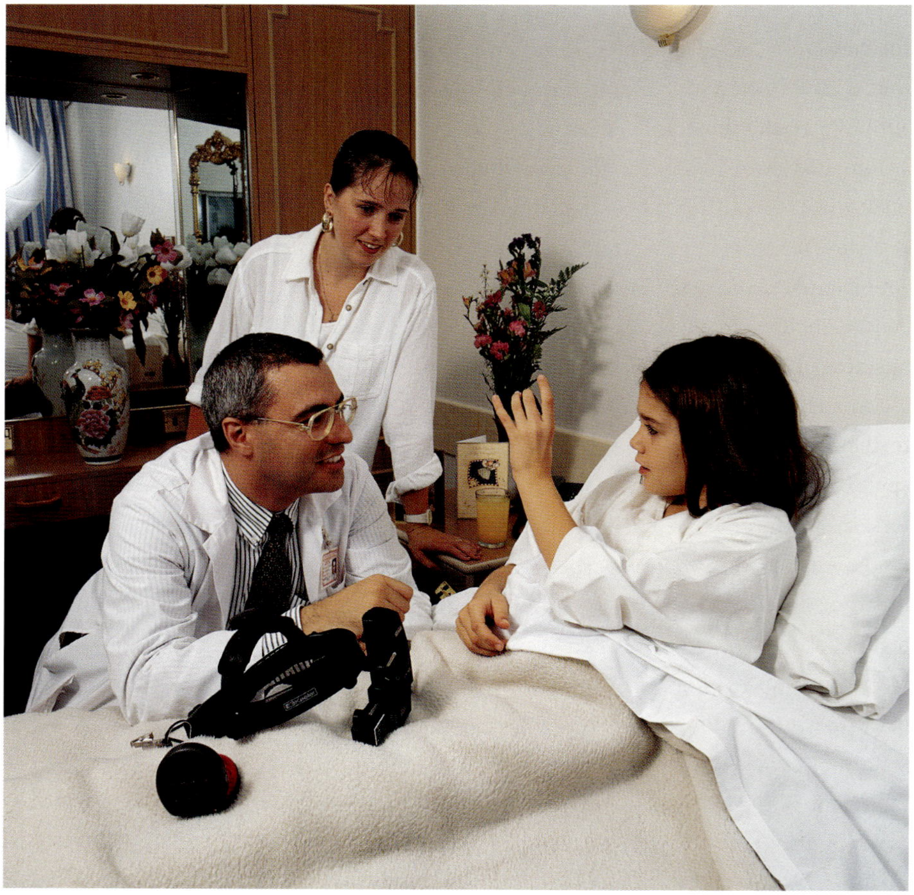

Medical care in Bahrain

porting implementing regulations, which were issued as Ministerial Order No. 6 of 1990. Prior to this, a number of laws had been looked upon as defining various aspects of the insurance environment, including the Labour Law of 1976 and subsequent amendments as they pertain to compensation for injury incurred in the course of employment and to social insurance to cover retirement benefits (both of which are handled by the General Organisation for Social Insurance – GOSI), and the Traffic Law of 1979 and later amendments, alluding to compulsory insurance for civil liability arising from traffic accidents.

It was to be Legislative Decree No. 17, however, which introduced for the first time the basis for the practice of insurance in the country including the appointment of the then Ministry of Commerce and Agriculture, today's Ministry of Commerce, to be the authority responsible for regulating and supervising the sector. The implementing regulations laid down the rules and regulations for establishing, licensing and registering insurance companies and organisations, the obligations of both the insured and the insurer in any insurance transaction, the necessity for the holding of reserves and deposits, the actions to be taken in the event an insurance company became subject to a merger or suspended trading and the level of annual fees payable to enable continued pursuit of the business in Bahrain, be the company a domestic or exempt, offshore, company.

In addition the rules and regulations for the practice of all other activities essential to the smooth running of the insurance industry were also addressed including those applicable to insurance experts, brokers and consultants, actuaries, surveyors, loss adjustors, insurance consultants and the opening and maintenance of representative offices.

In August 2002, insurance regulation and supervision was moved to the BMA. In fulfilling its new role the BMA has taken the opportunity to undertake a major review of the current regulatory framework applicable to insurance firms. In so doing it has sought substantial input from the Bahrain Insurance Association; has become a member of the International Association of Insurance Supervisors (IAIS); and, in April 2003, initiated the issuance of a series of consultation papers, the first of which addressed insurance captives.

The upgraded insurance legislation and regulations are likely to include specific definitions of both life and non-life insurance; the categories of insurance licence to be available and their specific terms, conditions and regulations; a revised minimum targeted paid-up capital requirement for locally established insurance companies; the definition of required solvency margins; and the need for both a compulsory statutory reserve, based on 10 per cent of annual net profit until the reserve reaches the equivalent of 100 per cent of paid-up capital, and a premium reserve. It is additionally anticipated that overall supervision of the insurance sector will be increased, with stronger penalties for transgressors; that the role of the insurance consultant and broker will be divided and more closely defined; and that individuals operating in the insurance sector will need to be qualified for the activity they are undertaking. Furthermore, a policyholders' protection fund is reportedly also under consideration.

In defining a new legislative and regulatory framework the BMA is seeking to build on its own existing infrastructure and consequently avoid duplication. For example, an extensive set of recommendations for dealing with money laundering and the financing of terrorism are already in place in the banking sector and will be used as a basis for developing appropriate requirements for insurers.

In establishing the new regulatory environment, the BMA is taking into consideration a very important document promulgated in late 2001, which makes a number of important pronouncements about insurance. Legislative Decree No. 19 of 2001 'with respect to the Promulgation of the Civil Code' lays down basic rights and responsibilities of both natural and juristic persons and, *inter alia*, gives prominence to the subject of insurance. Within the Code there is a clear definition of insurance, which is closely followed by a series of articles, 55 in total, addressing, among other details: the obligations of the parties to an insurance contract; a definition as to how insurance contracts are concluded; and a discourse on the transfer of the rights and obligations arising from such contracts. The document only addresses two specific classes of insurance, namely life and fire, but does have an impact across the whole insurance sector. As the definitive Civil Code of Bahrain, its authority is likely to be paramount in the introduction of new insurance legislation by the BMA.

Over the years the insurance sector has clearly been subject to a number of laws and regulations conducive to the effective transaction of its underlying activities. However, as the business of insurance becomes increasingly complex, the market for insurance services in Bahrain becomes more sophisticated and the BMA seeks to ensure the whole financial services sector complies with the most stringent international requirements, the introduction of a new regulatory and supervisory regime will serve to ensure full clarity in the practice of insurance in the Kingdom whilst enhancing the reputation of the sector not only within Bahrain but also in insurance and commercial circles worldwide.

The future of the insurance industry in Bahrain

The local insurance industry in Bahrain is already among the most developed in the region, with penetration rates also being higher than elsewhere in the Gulf. However, given Bahrain's membership of the WTO, the liberal commercial environment which prevails and the fact the BMA seems likely to look kindly on reputable companies seeking licences to set up in the country, significant growth potential for the industry is considered to remain.

To this end the BMA promotes and encourages the industry's development and has defined a number of objectives to be pursued:

- expansion of the domestic insurance industry;
- further development of Bahrain as a regional insurance centre;
- repositioning of the offshore sector;
- development of a regulatory and supervisory framework in close alignment with international standards.

Within the context of these objectives, the BMA is seeking to explore further bancassurance, Islamic insurance (*takaful*), reinsurance and captive insurance. It wishes also to give consideration to licensing those offshore insurance companies desirous of attaining onshore status by looking kindly on their applications given their capital is raised to the appropriate level and their operations are pursued in accordance with the laid down requirements. But first and foremost the Agency is looking to implement a regulatory regime fully compliant with the standards set by the IAIS, which is expected to be fully in place by the end of 2004.

9
Capital markets

To date, the principal emphasis in the Bahrain market, and within the GCC region as a whole, has been on the development of equity markets. Bahrain has played an important role to date in encouraging the development of an equity culture in the region and continues to push ahead towards fulfilling its potential. There are also hopes that in the longer term a large and liquid bond market will develop in the region. When it does, Bahrain's track record and expertise as a knowledge-based services hub will make the country the obvious centre of gravity for origination, distribution, sales, trading and research.

The Bahrain Stock Exchange (BSE)

Since the BSE began operations in 1989 it has grown to become one of the leading stock markets in the region. At the outset, 29 companies were listed, a figure which had grown to 40 as at end 2002, including the first non-Gulf Cooperation Council (GCC) company to be listed on any exchange in the region (a company from Sudan). Also listed are one Omani company, two from Kuwait and one from Qatar (for companies listed by sector see Appendix 5). Government bonds began to be quoted in 1994 and have risen in number from one that year to four as at 31 December 2002, with a number having been listed and repaid in the interim. Commercial bonds are also listed on the exchange, of which two remain, and mutual funds were first listed in 1995 when just one was quoted as compared with 33 as at the end of 2002.

History of the BSE

In the 1970s a local stock market existed in Bahrain, known as Al Jawhara Market, on which shares were traded informally over the counter and on a limited scale. This market was, to an extent, organised: share transactions could either be conducted through officially registered brokers, who in turn traded with a licensed dealer, or by direct dealings between investors. All such transactions were settled in cash and no share certificates were exchanged until such time as a settlement had been made in full. Some 20 public joint stock companies and 14 exempt companies were traded in this manner. Al Jawhara Market continued in operation until 1982.

However, events in Kuwait in 1982 when that country's unofficial share market, the Suq AlManakh, crashed, leaving many investors with heavy losses, focused the attention of the local authorities on the situation in Bahrain. Always aware of the need to protect investors and dealers alike, the Government looked closely at share trading in its own domestic market, which until this time had been governed solely by the Commercial Companies Law of 1975. As an interim measure, the Brokerage Law-Decree No.6 of 1982 and its interrelated regulations were introduced to provide added protection, whilst a comprehensive examination was made concerning the possible formation of a formal stock exchange.

A Stock Exchange Committee was formed under the chairmanship of the then Minister of Commerce and Agriculture. The Committee comprised representatives of the Ministry of Finance and National Economy, the BMA and the Bahrain Chamber of Commerce and Industry. It was charged with drawing up proposals for the establishment of an official stock exchange in Bahrain which would promote economic development in the country, ensure security for share dealers and promote confidence amongst investors and the general public.

Following research by the Stock Exchange Committee, and the preparation of a feasibility study in cooperation with the International Finance Corporation (IFC), Amiri Decree No. 4 of 1987 was promulgated, announcing the formation of the BSE, the by-laws for which were issued by Ministerial Decree in 1988. The Exchange began commercial operations a year later on 17 June 1989.

The primary objectives of the BSE were laid down by the decree and subsequently expanded upon in the by-laws. The main objectives from the outset have been to:

- develop the stock exchange in a way that helps the broader economic policy objectives of the State of Bahrain, by progressively developing the local exchange

Citibank dealing room

into a regional and international body and to facilitate the listing of non-Bahraini companies on the exchange and/or to accept dealing in their shares;

- encourage saving and promote investment awareness in the citizens with the objective of channelling their savings to productive sectors;
- develop and rationalise trading methods with a view to ensuring proper and sound dealings whilst providing proper protection for investors;
- develop the stock exchange so as to strengthen and reinforce the fiscal position of Bahrain by establishing relevant financial entities and introducing investment instruments to be traded on the exchange;

- regulate the procedures necessary for the issuing of stocks by companies seeking either a listing or an increase in their current level of capital;
- provide the necessary facilities conducive to the trading of local, regional or international stocks as determined by the board of directors;
- provide and raise capital to support and assist socioeconomic development;
- establish and develop contacts with regional and international exchanges and derive benefit from their dealing methods, thereby ensuring the progression to maturity of the local exchange.

The decree also determined that the BSE was to be administered by a board of directors comprising nine people under the chairmanship of the then Minister of Commerce and Agriculture, whose deputy would be a representative of the same ministry. Other board members were to be drawn from the Ministry of Finance and National Economy, the BMA, national banks and auditing firms (one from each) and three others nominated by the Bahrain Chamber of Commerce and Industry. The board members were to be appointed by the Council of Ministers upon the recommendation of the Minister of Commerce and Agriculture for renewable periods of three years. The day-to-day management of the BSE was vested in a director, again appointed by a ministerial edict upon the nomination of the Minister of Commerce and Agriculture, with an internal auditor, disciplinary board and arbitration committee reporting directly to the Board in support of the Exchange's activities.

Structure of the BSE

Following on from the appointment in August 2002 of the BMA as the regulator for the BSE as part of its overall regulatory mandate, a new board of directors of the Exchange was appointed in October the same year. Recognising the involvement of the BMA, the chairman and vice chairman are the governor and deputy governor of the BMA, which organisation also provides a further director. In addition, there are two representatives of the Bahrain Chamber of Commerce and Industry, a national bank representative and two representatives of brokerage companies in the market.

At inception, the BSE had just four departments, namely: Operations; Administration and Finance; Studies, Research and Development; and Control and Investigation. Since that time, the organisational structure of the BSE has grown and developed and today comprises the Operations, Information Technology, and

Exhibit 9.1: Organisational structure of the BSE

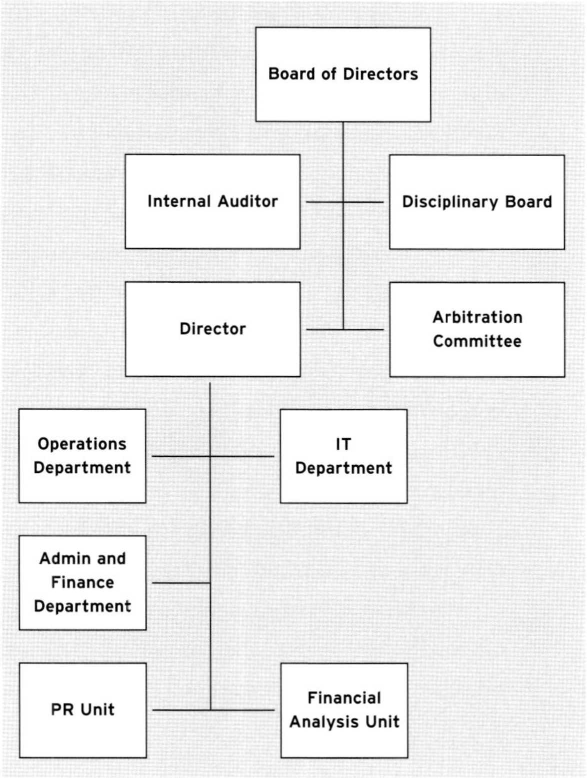

Administration and Finance departments plus two units for public relations and financial analysis (see Exhibit 9.1).

The main functions of these departments are:

- *Operations:* responsible for trading, clearing and settlement and central depository and for BSE's members' affairs;
- *Administration and Finance:* manages the financial resources of the BSE and administers staff in terms of recruitment, orientation and training. It also ensures that all transactions and deals are in accordance with the Exchange's rules and regulations;

- *Information Technology:* supports the BSE's computer systems and has responsibility for providing and updating the BSE with the latest technology. It operates the automated trading and clearing and settlement systems and develops in-house programs and applications, as and when required;
- *Financial Analysis and Information Unit:* conducts research and financial analysis of companies listed on the Exchange and also publishes statistical data, both current and historic. In addition, the Unit continually updates the financial information on the listed issues on the BSE;
- *Public Relations Unit:* promotes the BSE's activities and disseminates information to the public via newspapers, magazines and online media. It also organises exhibitions, road-shows and other promotional events whilst acting as the Exchange's liaison point with the public;
- *Arbitration Committee:* studies and settles all disputes relating to exchange transactions;
- *Disciplinary Board:* has powers to decide on any violation of the law, internal regulation or resolution which regulates the Exchange, and on any violation affecting the Exchange's conduct of business and discipline;
- *Internal Audit:* ensures that all departments comply with laws, regulations and rules, tests internal controls and evaluates management and operational risk.

Within the context of its objectives, the BSE sees its main role as the promotion of socioeconomic development through the provision of sound investment opportunities. Integral to this is the desire to increase the number of investors, to diversify the range of securities quoted on the exchange and to enhance cooperation between stock markets within the Middle East, thereby to ensure also the long-term development of the region's capital markets. To these ends, the BSE signed cross-listing agreements with the Muscat Securities Market in 1995; the Amman Financial Market in 1996; and the Egyptian Capital Market Authority a year later. Also in 1996 the BSE signed a tripartite agreement for cross-listing with the Kuwaiti and Omani exchanges and, in 1997, signed a linkage agreement with the Kuwait Stock Exchange to facilitate trading between the two countries.

Growth of the BSE

The early growth of unofficial share trading in Bahrain, before the BSE was established but following appointment of the Stock Exchange Committee, was based on a series of interim measures introduced on the directive of the Minister of Commerce and Agriculture. These were aimed at improving the levels and quality of share price information and, ultimately, at the introduction of a trading floor. To achieve this, an Information Centre was first established within the Ministry of Commerce and Agriculture. This centre was linked to all registered brokers who, on completing a trade, notified the centre, which in turn recorded the details and relayed price and volume details to all the other brokers simultaneously. At the end of each day a summary of all transactions was forwarded to all brokers and to the local media for publication.

This centre was also responsible for ensuring the availability and timely dissemination of price sensitive information and for ensuring that all companies whose shares were quoted on the exchange provided all necessary information likely to impact on investment decision-making and market prices.

In the mid-1980s the economies of the wider Middle East, including that of Bahrain, all suffered a marked set-back resulting from a fall in world oil prices. The government sought, therefore, to revive the domestic economy, at least in part, through the introduction of a number of remedial measures for the stock exchange. These were announced in August 1986, came into force early in 1987, and were aimed at encouraging enhanced trading in shares. They comprised:

- approval for nationals of other GCC countries to own up to 25 per cent of the shares of Bahrain public joint stock companies;
- approval for public joint stock companies to purchase up to 5 per cent of their own issued shares;
- granting the legal right to companies to issue preference shares; and
- approval for the General Organisation for Social Insurance (GOSI) and for civil and military pension funds to own up to 10 per cent of any one company's issued shares.

When the BSE began trading there were two categories of securities: 'listed' and 'admitted to trading', all of which were shares of Bahraini public joint stock companies, although the listing and trading of government and corporate bonds, as well as other debt securities, was also permitted. From the beginning membership of the BSE comprised individual and corporate stockbrokers and market-makers and any other individual or corporate body granted membership by the exchange's board.

The introduction of the BSE had an immediately positive affect. In its first year of operation total turnover amounted to 61.3 million shares valued at BD14.3 million (US$37.9 million). In addition, transfers of 1.6 million shares with a value of BD950,000 were recorded in 64 exempt cases (transactions which are permitted off the trading floor under the terms of Article 36 of the BSE by-laws). In 1990 the total volume of shares reached 98.5 million, with a value of BD33.7 million. The value of exempt cases (totalling 326) was 54.7 million shares with a value of BD23.23 million, and BD6.5 million worth of shares were sold in a local hotel company by the government.

Encouraged by the successes of its formative years, the BSE soon moved to broaden the scope of its activities with the basic aim of promoting yet further interest in the trading of shares. Integral to this initiative were the listing of the shares issued by the Arab Banking Corporation, when raising its capital in 1990, and the permission granted to non-GCC investors to trade in them and then in the shares of three exempt companies quoted on the Exchange: Bahrain International Bank, Investcorp Bank and TAIB Bank (listed in 1994). This action placed the BSE to the fore in the GCC in allowing non-GCC nationals to trade on a local exchange. Subsequently, it became permissible for non-Bahraini residents of Bahrain, as well as other foreigners, to invest in local shares subject to clearly defined limits, which had now grown to a maximum shareholding of 49 per cent by GCC nationals and 24 per cent by other nationals.

After the BSE's first eight years of steady growth the board of directors initiated a more aggressive strategy: the exchange would be developed and expanded to attract a greater number of investors and increase yet further the level of trading on the market. The primary elements of this new strategy were the strengthening of the legal infrastructure, the adoption of fully automated trading and related systems, the enhancement of the level of training provided to employees and the upgrading of the quality of marketing and promotion of the BSE.

In 1999 this new strategy was successfully implemented. One of the first elements to be put into practice was the further opening up of the stock market to foreign investors, with GCC nationals now being permitted, under the terms of Resolution No. 10 of 1999, to own up to 100 per cent of the equity of a BSE-quoted company and other nationalities 49 per cent, an effective doubling of the previous limits. This move contributed positively as the share of foreign ownership of companies listed on the BSE as at 31 May 2003 exceeded that of local ownership – at 49.07 per cent for non-Bahraini GCC nationals and 7.64 per cent for other nationalities. Another important element of the strategy implemented was to allow foreign brokers to operate in Bahrain, a move

Exhibit 9.2: Trading history of the BSE, 1989-December 2002

Period	*BSE Index*	*Market capitalisation (BD)*	*Shares traded (value, BD)*	*Shares traded (volume, no of shares)*	*Share turnover % (value)*	*Shareholders' equity (BD)*
1989		1,120,697,914	14,342,129	61,286,888	1.28	
1990	1,046.39	1,196,761,665	33,671,557	98,466,653	2.82	1,194,986,930
1991	1,430.45	1,549,302,019	39,535,390	78,126,326	2.55	1,290,479,180
1992	1,509.42	1,657,794,895	63,104,996	189,998,891	3.83	1,315,662,109
1993	1,928.31	2,120,238,767	96,446,015	389,556,968	4.55	1,419,906,650
1994	1,518.93	1,879,677,464	60,398,882	257,179,593	3.20	1,491,323,468
1995	1,326.56	1,779,936,591	39,994,158	184,726,834	2.25	1,613,836,331
1996	1,547.35	1,896,898,687	66,568,287	298,837,238	3.51	1,717,999,697
1997	2,310.09	2,954,876,062	180,766,187	630,059,899	6.13	2,029,041,429
1998	2,188.92	2,553,285,354	217,298,302	619,736,211	8.51	2,096,325,433
1999	2,212.20	2,699,595,175	167,955,369	536,285,913	6.22	2,155,636,891
2000	1,805.76	2,497,379,687	92,531,838	422,073,412	3.71	2,413,092,014
2001	1,761.45	2,484,680,694	72,209,717	335,280,948	2.90	2,505,287,259
2002	1,821.48	2,850,493,851	77,767,740	352,909,791	2.73	2,501,450,904

Source: Bahrain Stock Exchange.

designed to ensure improved expertise and overall standards on the BSE in line with the board's aspirations.

Also in 1999, the BSE's automated trading system was introduced, to be followed in due course by the automated clearing, settlement, depository and registration system. The introduction of this new technology meant that substantial attention had to be paid to the BSE's legal infrastructure leading to the introduction or amendment of many rules and regulations.

Market capitalisation has increased over the 14 years since inception of the exchange from BD1.12 billion (US$2.97 billion) in the first year of operations to BD2.85 billion (US$7.6 billion) in December 2002 (see Exhibit 9.2), peaking in 1997 at BD2.95 billion (US$7.82 billion). This represents an average annual growth rate of 10.7 per cent. Trading volume also peaked in 1997 at 630.1 million shares, subsequently declining over the succeeding three years to a low of 335.3 million shares as the national economy faced somewhat straightened circumstances in the face of falling oil prices. The value of trades peaked a year later, in 1998, at BD217.3 million (US$579.5 million),

Exhibit 9.3: BSE Index, 1989-2002

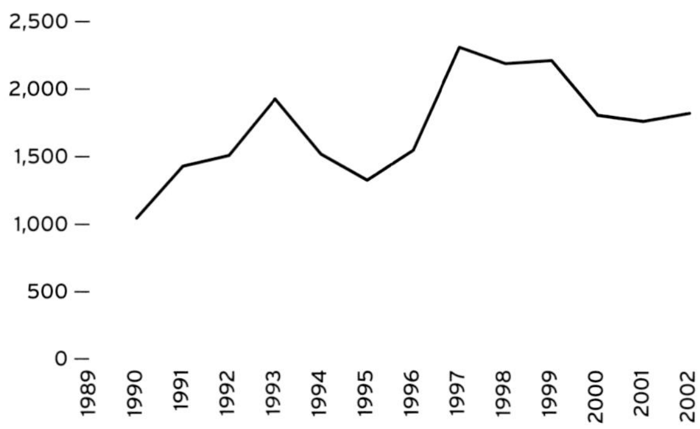

Source: Bahrain Stock Exchange, Financial Analysis and Information Unit.

Exhibit 9.4: Shares turnover, 1989-2002 (%)

Source: Bahrain Stock Exchange, Financial Analysis and Information Unit.

Exhibit 9.5: Market capitalisation, 1989-2002 (BD million)

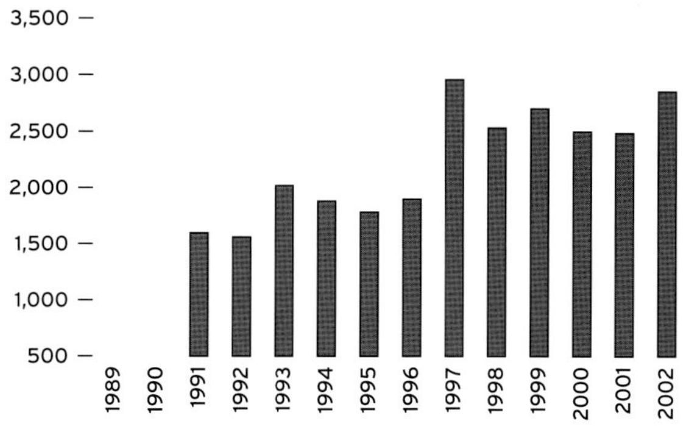

Source: Bahrain Stock Exchange, Financial Analysis and Information Unit.

Exhibit 9.6: Value, 1989-2002 (BD million)

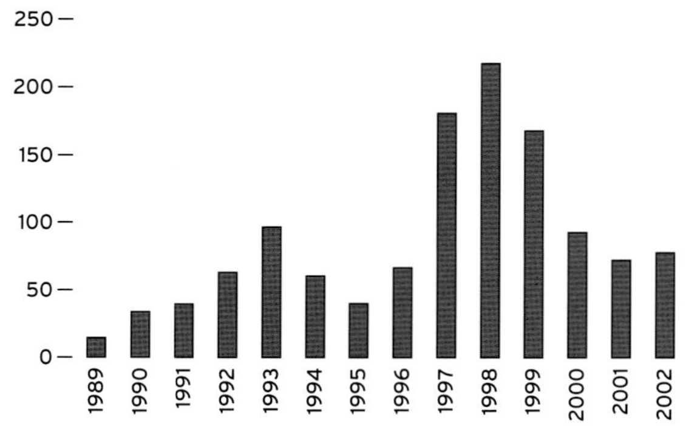

Source: Bahrain Stock Exchange, Financial Analysis and Information Unit.

Exhibit 9.7: Volume, 1989-2002 (Shares, million)

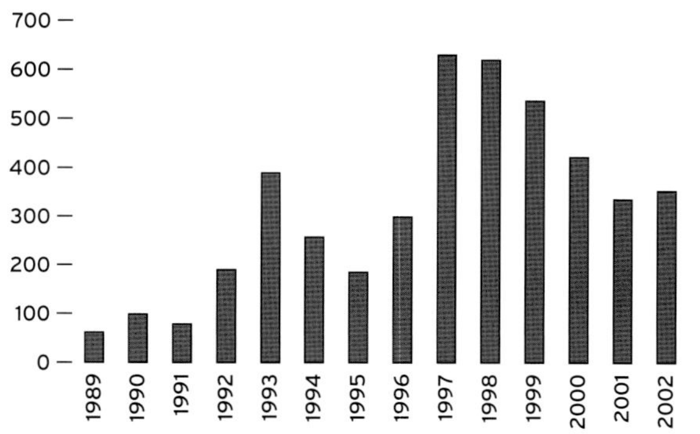

Source: Bahrain Stock Exchange, Financial Analysis and Information Unit.

Exhibit 9.8: Shareholders' equity, 1989-2002 (BD million)

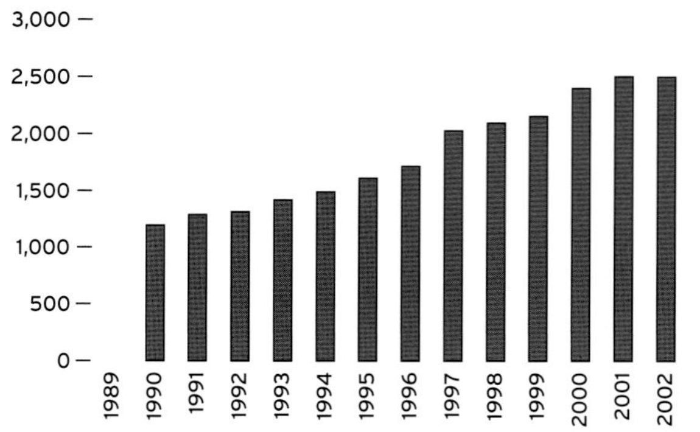

Source: Bahrain Stock Exchange, Financial Analysis and Information Unit.

a figure which subsequently fell away dramatically to BD72.2 million (US$192.5 million) in 2001. Subsequently, in 2002, growth, albeit limited, in both volume and value was again seen when 352.9 million shares, valued at BD77.8 million (US$207.5 million), were traded. This upward move took place in the early days of enhanced prosperity in Bahrain arising in part out of increased oil revenues, the initiation of a number of major developmental projects in the country, the first steps taken in implementing democratic processes, including the introduction of municipal and government elections, and increased confidence amongst consumers.

Exhibits 9.2 to 9.8 show that while shareholders' equity has seen steady growth over the 12 years covered, with a slight dip in 2002, the remaining indicators have shown not inconsiderable fluctuation. These are largely the result of movements in the world oil price and their impact on the economic and political atmosphere in the Gulf region. Even the Gulf War in late 1990 and early 1991, seems not to have had a major impact as, with the exception of the volume of shares traded and the value of shares turned over, all the indices evidenced continued growth. With the prevailing optimism in Bahrain, for the reasons given above, the potential is perceived to exist for the market to move out of its extended period of consolidation onto an upward growth path.

The BSE composite index currently comprises six sectoral indices representing 24 companies. These are as follows: commercial banks (five), investment (four), insurance (three), services (seven companies covering trading, telecommunications, ship repair, duty free services and car parks), industries (two) and hotel and tourism (three).

Government bonds

Alongside shares the BSE also lists both government and corporate bonds. Exhibit 9.9 shows the number of bonds listed historically since their first years of trading. The bonds quoted as at December 2002 are shown in Exhibit 9.10.

As well as government bonds, which may be conventional bonds or *sukuk al-ijarah*, Islamic bonds, a number of corporate bonds have been issued over past years of which just two – for Bahrain Commercial Facilities Company, with a value of BD15 million – remain outstanding. This follows the repayment of US$100 million (BD37.7 million) of bonds for Aluminium Bahrain on their maturity in 2001.

Most bonds are taken up by commercial banks, GOSI, the Pension Fund Commission, semi-governmental institutions and private sector companies. They

Exhibit 9.9: Bonds traded, 1994-2002

Year	*Bonds listed during the year*	*Bonds de-listed during the year*	*Bonds listed up to 30 Dec 2002*
1994	2		2
1995			2
1996			2
1997	1	1	2
1998	1		3
1999	1		4
2000	1	1	4
2001	2	1	5
2002	2		7

Source: Bahrain Stock Exchange.

Exhibit 9.10: Bonds quoted, as at December 2002

Issue	*Amount of issue (million)*	*Maturity*	*Yield to maturity (%)*
Bahrain government fixed rate bond	BD40	2003	6.250
Long-term government bonds	BD100	2029	2.3700
BCFC* bonds (third issue)	BD8	2005	5.0000
BCFC* bonds (fourth issue)	BD7	2006	5.0000
Islamic leasing *sukuk*	US$100	2006	5.25
Islamic leasing *sukuk* (second issue)	US$70	2005	4.25
Islamic leasing *sukuk* (third issue)	US$80	2007	4.00

*Bahrain Commercial Facilities Company.

Source: Bahrain Stock Exchange.

tend to be held by their purchasers to maturity, due in large part to the relatively high yield which they provide. Thus the secondary bond market is very limited. However, the BMA does provide a facility known as the discount window facility whereby up to the full amount of a conventional government bond may be discounted by its holder for one of three periods – overnight, two days and seven days. The interest charged on such transactions differs from time to time but tends to be higher than the repo rate charged against Treasury bills. Such a facility is not, however, available against an Islamic *sukuk al-ijarah*, although these leasing certificates do have a wide appeal not just among the Muslim community, but also among conventional banks and financial institutions.

Foreign bonds may also be listed on the BSE subject to clearly defined terms, including issuance in accordance with the laws of their country of origin and subsequent approval by the BMA. No such bonds were quoted on the BSE as of December 2002.

Looking to the future

The BSE has in recent years reinforced all its rules, regulations and standards to be fully in accordance with international practice ensuring the market enjoys an improved level of transparency and efficiency thereby enhancing investors' confidence in the market and the higher level of protection afforded to investors. In August 2002 the BSE ceased to be self-regulatory when responsibility for all regulation and supervision passed to the Capital Markets Supervision Directorate at the BMA, which oversees and monitors its activities.

As the market moves forward into the twenty-first century, the BSE will be increasingly prepared for the anticipated developments in the marketplace, including the possibility of initial public offerings (IPOs) of major companies, not just in Bahrain but Gulf-wide; the privatisation of entities such as utilities, telecommunications and airlines in the region; mergers between existing quoted companies; and cross-listing of securities between regional exchanges and possibly those from further afield.

The advanced Clearing, Settlement and Central Depository System (CDS) is being monitored to ensure the exchange maintains its position as a leader in the introduction of technologically advanced systems. As at end September 2002, 1.3 billion shares, 16.81 per cent of all outstanding shares on the Exchange, had been deposited in the system by 1,200 investors from over 20 countries. These figures show clearly that the system has gained quick acceptance.The Guarantee Fund, contributed to by brokers in case of a member's failure or inability to make settlement, will also be overseen to ensure proper adequacy levels as the market grows, and on-line trading, which became a reality for the BSE in 2003, picks up.

As to the future there is the likelihood of an interrelated Islamic Capital Market being introduced, as is the full privatisation of the BSE. The future augurs well for the BSE, which is well placed to derive maximum benefits from the opportunities increasingly certain to be available.

Funds management

Mutual funds

Collective investment schemes, under which banner unit trusts and mutual funds are recognised by the BMA, first became regulated in Bahrain in 1992 as an integral element of a move to develop and diversify Bahrain as an international financial centre.

In essence, the regulation passed at that time introduced a simple and flexible yet comprehensive set of rules and regulations for the approval, authorisation, supervision and marketing of collective investment schemes and responded, in part at least, to the requests of the international financial community, and specifically fund managers, who had expressed an interest in being able to establish and to market such schemes both in and from Bahrain.

The regulation provides a clear definition as to what is meant by a 'collective investment scheme', which is not dissimilar to that used in other jurisdictions, and takes into account all the necessary prudential principles and best practice appropriate to all well-managed fund management centres, including those within the G10 countries. In formulating the regulation, full attention has been given to the EC's UCITS (Undertakings for Collective Investment and Transferable Securities) Regulations of 1989, which lay down a number of important criteria relating to collective investment schemes. The regulation also grants the BMA the right to make subsidiary rules and regulations on an as-needed basis and to issue new principles of supervision, operation and marketing for the proper and regular enforcement of schemes.

As a result, every collective investment scheme must be approved individually and only those schemes fully approved and authorised by the BMA may be established in or marketed from Bahrain. Furthermore, they may only be marketed by banks or financial institutions that have been licensed by the BMA and therefore maintain a presence in Bahrain. It is the case, however that the money changers are specifically excluded from this activity.

In the initial two-year period following issuance of the regulation, approval and authorisation had been given to 26 banks and financial institutions to establish and market 186 schemes. By 1997 those figures had increased to 31 banks and 300 funds and by the end of March 2003 to some 50 banks and financial institutions and 1,478 schemes. This latter figure has arisen in part from a readjustment to the BMA's recognition of umbrella funds, which had been looked upon formerly as single funds but which are now deemed to be separate funds beneath the umbrella. As of March 2003 the total assets of licensed funds exceeded US$3.98 billion, with 33 funds being locally incorporated and with an asset value of US$504 million.

Prior to licensing mutual funds, the BMA makes exhaustive enquiries as to their provenance and especially their management. However, funds for which licensing in Bahrain is sought and which are registered within a well-regulated authority in their country of origin are likely to be accepted without undue delay.

Of the funds licensed in Bahrain, 37 are Islamic funds, with assets of US$130 million, included amongst which is the first Iranian mutual fund to be offered to investors outside Iran, and which is registered in Bahrain. The regulation of Islamic funds is not dissimilar to that for conventional funds although the underlying assets are likely to differ. Many Islamic funds include *murabaha* transactions in their portfolios (see Chapter 6 on Islamic finance and banking) alongside those international equities that are perceived not to contravene Islamic principles – predominantly those equities included in the six Dow Jones Islamic Market Indices.

Of the total funds licensed only a limited number are quoted on the BSE. As at the end of December 2002 just 28 funds were so listed, a number which had increased by 7 from the end of the previous year (see Exhibit 9.11). The listing of mutual funds on the BSE is not obligatory but has become a way of providing their issuers with expo-

Exhibit 9.11: Mutual funds listed, 1995–2002

Year	*Funds listed during the year*	*No of funds listed up to year end*	*No of funds de-listed during the year*
1995	1	1	-
1996	1	2	-
1997	1	3	-
1998	18	21	-
1999	13	34	-
2000	13	39	*8
2001	1	21	**19
2002	7	28	-

* 7 Discontinued, I final redemption.
**Discontinued.

Source: Bahrain Stock Exchange.

Exhibit 9.12: Mutual funds - total outstanding investments, 2000 and 2001 (US$ '000s)

Year (31 Dec)	*Type of bank*	*Investors: institutions*	*Investors: individuals*	*Total amount invested in the funds*
2000	Full commercial bank	55,458	185,091	241,549
	Offshore banking units	56,094	34,169	90,263
	Investment banks	1,010,071	328,435	1,338,506
	Representative offices	307,938	27,306	335,244
	Other Institutions	1,861	187	2,048
	Total	1,432,422	575,188	2,007,610
2001	Full commercial bank	75,558	168,451	244,009
	Offshore banking units	68,172	43,464	111,636
	Investment banks	1,686,044	530,095	2,216,139
	Representative offices	204,242	37,593	241,835
	Other Institutions	15,400	1,284	16,684
	Total	2,049,416	780,887	2,830,303
2002	Full commercial banks	53,544	539,212	592,756
	Offshore banking units	374,68	151,151	425,832
	Investment banks	1,620,761	560,670	2,181,431
	Representative offices	319,428	141,591	461,019
	Other Institutions	363,858	9,618	373,476
	Total	2,732,272	1,302,242	4,034,514

Source: BMA - Quarterly Statistical Bulletins, December 2001 and 2002.

sure to potential clients for their ranges of funds. No trading of mutual funds takes place on the market.

The BMA has ambitions to make Bahrain an increasingly reputable international centre for collective investment schemes and, whilst ensuring a strict regulatory and supervisory environment, has minimised the legal and licensing requirements for funds in the country, has confirmed the absence of taxation on either trusts or their clients and has sought also to ensure that Bahrain is cheaper than other international financial centres where such funds are registered.

Financial trusts

These were first regulated in Bahrain in June 1998 with the primary objective of attracting more trust funds to the islands. However few trusts have so far been formed under the existing regulations and the BMA is actively examining the possibility of enhancing the existing regulatory and supervisory environment with the ultimate aim of ensuring the confidence of the international community in using Bahrain as a location in which to register trusts.

The concept of a trust is not well-known in the Muslim world as the devolution of family-owned assets is clearly defined under Islamic law and effectively precludes the use of trusts for elective devolution of assets. It is the case, however, that a corporate entity could use a trust, for example, for employee benefit and share option schemes or an off-balance sheet structure for holding shares and assets. As businesses in the region cease to be family owned – a slow process but one which is taking place – these possibilities are likely to have an increasing importance.

When the BMA first introduced its regulation in regard to trusts, its prime intention had been to standardise and control the practices of banks and other financial institutions in Bahrain that provided trust-based banking and financial products, while providing a coherent structure to enable financial institutions licensed by the BMA to set up and market a wide range of trust-based financial instruments, especially, but not exclusively, investment trusts and other tax-efficient investment devices. The BMA continues to develop the concept further.

Regulation

Until 1987 the then existing stock market was largely regulated by the Ministry of Commerce and Agriculture but once the BSE was formed, and while it remained under the aegis of the Ministry, the BSE became largely self-regulatory. This was encouraged from the outset when the BSE's Board of Directors was formed of both governmental and private sector representatives, who were chosen for their ability to contribute to the BSE those administrative and commercial skills required to meet the Exchange's regulatory and supervisory needs.

Since then, the rules and regulations applicable have been based largely on the Commercial Companies Law, with which all listed companies must fully comply, and the BSE's own internal by-laws and directives.. To ensure compliance, the BSE maintained at that time its own Legal Affairs and Inspection Department, which in earlier days was known as the Monitoring and Investigation Department, which was in a position to ask the Board of Directors to take action in regard to suspicious transactions by suspending temporarily trading of a company. Should a full suspension ensue this could only have resulted from a resolution of the Minister of Commerce and Industry. To ensure proper conduct of all investigations, both an arbitration panel and a disciplinary board existed, one member of each of which must be a judge appointed by the Ministry of Justice and Islamic Affairs.

Integral to the Board's activities are the laying down of rules governing the trading of securities, the listing of shares of local and foreign joint stock companies, or other securities, and also the registration of stockbrokers. In this latter regard, all brokers and market-makers must satisfy the standards laid down by the Board, which seek to ensure their ability and suitability to conduct business professionally in accordance with established principles. Brokers, for example, must hold the Investment Representative Programme Certificate, which is equivalent to the Securities and Exchange Commission (SEC) Series 7 qualification required by brokers in the United States before they are allowed to trade.

Over the years, the BSE has sought consistently to reinforce the Exchange's rules and regulations to ensure their concordance with best international practice, largely by ensuring that they are akin to those applied by the SEC in the United States. It has endeavoured also to evolve and upgrade the standards and procedures in place to ensure transparency, full disclosure and investor protection. The BSE has prepared a set of disclosure-based regulations based on IOSCO (International Organization for Securities Commissions) standards, which are undoubtedly the most comprehensive and advanced in the region. All companies listed on the exchange must comply fully with International Accounting Standards (IAS).

Since August 2002, the BSE has officially been under the aegis of the BMA and therefore subject to the regulatory and supervisory environment created by the new single regulator. This situation undoubtedly serves to enhance the already well-regulated and supervised BSE to the ultimate benefit of listed companies and investors alike.

10
Formation and functioning of the money market

Introduction

All licensed banks in Bahrain, including full commercial banks, OBUs and investment banks are permitted by the BMA to deal freely with each other and with financial institutions in other centres in both Bahraini dinars and foreign currency. In pursuit of their money market activities, the banks may deal also with the four money brokers registered in the islands.

Until the early 1970s there had been only minimal money market activity in Bahrain due in part to Bahrain's membership of the Sterling Area, the modest affluence of the country and the nature of international communications at that time, which did not permit the speed of transaction essential in the markets today. But then in 1973 the rapid rise in world oil prices led to a boom in the economy and the government, businesses and wealthy individuals alike all began to seek alternatives to placing their funds on deposit with the local banks.

Shortly after this, in 1975, the crisis in Lebanon caused many bankers to leave that country and some came to Bahrain where the excess liquidity of Saudi Arabia, by far the largest source of funds, could be handled. In turn this attracted the money brokers, the first of whom arrived in 1975 with the others being licensed between then and 1979, and a genuine money market began to develop, which also benefited from the country's location mid-way between London and the markets of South-East Asia.

The Saudi riyal became and remained the most important currency traded and Bahrain remains to this day the major centre for trading in that currency. Indeed it is suggested that 60 per cent of all OBUs' business is in that currency. Initially there was only a spot market in the Saudi riyal, but over time the whole market changed such that today some 90 per cent of all Saudi riyal business is in the forward market, usually for one, three and six months or, as an absolute maximum, one year.

The Bahraini dinar market

The Bahraini dinar interbank market is dominated by the full commercial banks, which are the only financial institutions in Bahrain permitted to accept deposits from their local customers, be they companies or individuals. Three other factors also impinge on the commercial banks' availability of dinars – the public's demand for notes and coins; the commercial banks' purchases of US dollars from the BMA; and the conversion by the government of the country's oil revenues from US dollars to dinars to fund domestic expenditure. In this latter regard it is usually the case that the government sells its dollars to the BMA and then places the dinars resulting from the exchange with local commercial banks. Hence the commercial banks' ready availability of dinars for lending, not only to their customers but also to other commercial banks and to the OBUs, which tend to be in the market more as borrowers of the dinar to fund their dinar assets, including local currency securities and loans to non-residents and residents, where the latter has been authorised by the BMA. Despite the ready availability of dinars they tend to be used largely for the reasons given, which minimises any activity in the currency on the local money market.

A substantial majority of borrowings in the dinar tend to be of short duration, overnight or to seven days. Importantly, the BMA does act as lender of last resort in the dinar market on an as-required basis and thus is always ready to provide the local commercial banks with funds they are unable to source from the market.

In the past, and until 1987, the BMA provided the local commercial banks with liquidity under swap arrangements against the US dollar, usually for periods of seven days, but sometimes overnight. The rate of interest charged was very much of the BMA's own choosing. Also in earlier years domestic market liquidity was enhanced by the discounting of Aluminium Bahrain promissory notes and also by providing a lending window against government development bonds. Since 1987, however, all such assistance has been provided through sale and repurchase (repo) of Bahrain Government Treasury bills.

BMA dealing room

Treasury bills have been issued by the BMA on behalf of the Government since December 1986, the first time a country within the GCC region had taken such an initiative. Their issuance was integral to the Government's need for short-term finance and to promote the development of a domestic money market by providing the banks and investors with a marketable instrument by which to absorb excess dinar liquidity.

Treasury bills are issued, following auctions organised by the BMA, on a weekly basis for a maturity of 91 days and on a monthly basis for a maturity of 182 days.

Exhibit 10.1: Details of the last 10 auctions to 31 January 2003 are provided as indicators of the demand for Treasury bills

Date of issue 2002/03	*Total tenders received (BD million)*	*Treasury bills allotted (BD million)*	*Average price of bills allotted %*	*Average internal rate of allotted bills (% pa)*	*BD Intermarket 3 to 6 month offered rate*
I December	9.50	5.00	99.325	1.35	1.62
4 December	23.10	10.00	99.671	1.31	1.50
18 December	16.50	10.00	99.667	1.32	1.50
22 December	6.70	5.00	99.297	1.40	1.62
25 December	13.90	10.00	99.672	1.30	1.50
2 January	14.90	10.00	99.676	1.30	1.50
15 January	37.20	10.00	99.674	1.29	1.50
19 January	9.00	5.00	99.310	1.37	1.62
22 January	32.80	10.00	99.676	1.29	1.43
29 January	28.00	10.00	99.681	1.27	1.43

Source: BMA-Quarterly Statistical Bulletin, December 2002.

The bills are interest free, being issued at a discount to parity or repayment value with the difference between the issue and nominal value being the return due to the investor.

Tenders for the Treasury bills may be made by commercial banks in Bahrain, some government agencies, and resident companies and individuals. However, companies and individuals must make their offers through the banks.

Over the years tenders, of which 950 issues had been made as of early June 2003, have consistently exceeded the value of bills on offer and so the BMA has regularly been able to allot bills on a competitive basis according to the prices offered by the tendering institutions. Subsequent to any auction, the BMA publishes full details of the total value of the tenders received, the average allotment price, the average yield-to-maturity of the bills issued and the minimum tender price accepted. As at 31 January 2003 the value of Treasury bills outstanding amounted to BD160 million (US$428 million) (see Exhibit 10.1). The secondary market in Treasury bills is very limited as successful bidders tend to hold them to maturity.

More recently, the BMA has started to issue *sukuk al-salam* (about which more detail is provided under Islamic banks and Islamic finance in Chapter 6) which are, in

Exhibit 10.2: Domestic public debt instruments

Conventional instruments[1]

End of period	Development bonds[3]			Treasury bills[4]			Outstanding balance
	Matured	*New issue*	*Balance*	*Matured*	*New issue*	*Balance*	
1998	36.0	56.0	157.0	620.0	685.0	225.0	382.0
1999	40.0	140.0	257.0	840.0	840.0	225.0	482.0
2000	-	100.0	357.0	655.0	650.0	220.0	577.0
2001	40.0	-	317.0	600.0	570.0	190.0	507.0
2002	21.0	-	296.0	520.0	490.0	160.0	456.0

Islamic instruments[2]

End of period	Islamic leasing securities[5]			Al Salam Islamic securities[6]			Outstanding balance	Grand total
	Matured	*New issue*	*Balance*	*Matured*	*New issue*	*Balance*		
1998	-	-	-	-	-	-	-	382.0
1999	-		-	-	-	-	-	482.0
2000	-	-		-	-	-	-	577.0
2001	-	37.6	37.6	37.6	65.8	28.2	65.8	572.8
2002	-	75.2	112.8	112.8	112.8	28.2	141.0	597.0

[1] Conventional instruments are issued in Bahraini Dinars
[2] Islamic instruments are issued in US dollars.
[3] Development bonds have a maturity of 5 years and 30 years.
[4] Treasury bills have a maturity of 91 days, 182 days and one year.
[5] Islamic leasing securities have a maturity of 5 years.
[6] Al Salam Islamic securities have a maturity of 91 days.

Source: Bahrain Monetary Agency, *Quarterly Statistical Bulletin*, 31 December 2002.

effect, an Islamic form of Treasury bill but which are not available for discount due to the absence, at the present time, of a discount mechanism not interrelated with interest (see Exhibit 10.2).

Bahraini dinar certificates of deposit

Certificates of deposit (CDs) in the dinar may be issued by the local commercial banks with a minimum value of BD30,000 for periods between six months and five years. CDs may be issued to other banks or to customers and must be freely negotiable under the terms of Bahraini law. As with Treasury bills, the secondary market in CDs tends to be very thin, with holders usually retaining them to maturity.

Eurobond market

A Bahraini dinar Eurobond market was permitted to open by the BMA in 1977 and in that year and 1978 five issues with a value of BD49 million (US$130 million) were made, by countries as disparate as Mexico and Algeria. All five issues were option bonds with payments and coupons being payable in both dinars and US dollars; were in bearer form with interest payable annually; and were free from withholding tax.

Since that time no further dinar-denominated Eurobonds have been issued, partly due to the BMA's regulations that any such issue will only be approved provided the proceeds are used for development projects in Bahrain and that the borrowing would not lead to an outflow from the BMA's foreign exchange reserves on maturity should the dinar proceeds be converted into foreign currency.

The offshore and investment banks are regular participants in international Eurobond issues and in trading them in the course of their market dealings. Some of the banks have bond trading departments and have become market-makers, especially in floating rate notes.

Financial futures and derivatives

There is no international financial futures exchange in Bahrain but a number of banks and other financial institutions are active in the futures markets, predominantly on behalf of their clients. But the business is generally small.

Derivatives such as interest rate swaps, options and future rate agreements are all used, especially Saudi riyal interest rate swaps, which might be for periods of between two and five years and often priced off the back of the US dollar. But, again, the market is only modest.

Syndicated loans

Bahrain-based banks are active participants in the syndicated loans market both as lead managers and participants. Particular success has been achieved in this regard in obtaining mandates to arrange loans for both sovereign and corporate borrowers in the region. A number of banks have also acted as agent bank for syndicated loans.

Outlook

The potential exists for the Bahraini money market to grow and develop further as part of the Kingdom's capital market becoming increasingly important as a regional centre. Developments in banking throughout the GCC are moving into an important phase where local and regional banks are seeking increasingly to deal amongst themselves so developing a larger local market in regional and international currencies, of which the Saudi riyal and the US dollar remain the most important. Furthermore, as the regional banks become more involved in areas such as project and structured financing so they are working together more closely. Over time, this situation is likely to enhance the status of the regional money market in Bahrain, especially given its regulation and supervision by the BMA and provided it continues to be innovative.

11 Depositor and creditor protection

Introduction

The BMA, in undertaking its regulatory role, seeks primarily to ensure the banking profession and banking system operate according to international standards, thus ensuring the stability of the financial system and instilling confidence in those using the services. The BMA's success in carrying out this role is borne out by the reputation that Bahrain has earned as an international financial centre.

To ensure Bahrain maintains its status as a safe destination for a wide range of financial activities, the BMA has been especially keen to provide security for customers and investors in what has become an increasingly competitive and sophisticated financial environment. So the BMA has introduced an effective Deposit Protection Scheme specifically aimed at smaller depositors in the locally established commercial banks. In addition, a set of regulatory practices has been introduced offering protection to investors seeking to benefit from the investment and financial advisory services available in the Kingdom.

At the same time the BMA wishes to provide maximum protection to banks, corporate entities and private individuals in carrying out their normal business with full confidence in the financial system. So it has introduced to the banking system a number of safeguards against credit risks and unpaid, returned cheques.

Establishment of the Deposit Protection Scheme

To ensure the protection of bank customers and in accordance with Resolution No. 3

of 1993, the BMA issued a Regulation in July 1994 concerning the establishment of a Deposit Protection Scheme and a Deposit Protection Board.

One of the aims of the Scheme is to protect all depositors, but especially small depositors, against the risk of insolvency of full commercial banks in Bahrain. It seeks to ensure immediate and sufficient compensation is made to depositors in the event of any insolvency or bankruptcy of a locally established bank without waiting for the liquidation process to be completed.

The Deposit Protection Scheme applies to specified deposits, which include funds on current, call, savings or fixed deposit accounts or holders of non-bearer certificates of deposit denominated in Bahraini dinars or any other currency held with the Bahrain offices of a full commercial bank by any person, whether resident or not. The Scheme specifically proscribes benefit being derived by the Bahrain Government or its agencies; other banks; parents, subsidiaries, associates or affiliates of the insolvent bank; directors, shareholders with more than a 5 per cent shareholding or managers of the insolvent bank; persons whose identity cannot be positively ascertained; owners of deposits that have been illegally obtained and/or relate to illicit matters; and/or holders of deposits that are subject to any charge or lien, whether general or specific, or right of set-off by the insolvent bank.

The benefit to be derived under the Scheme by any depositor is limited to a maximum of the lesser of 75 per cent of the combined total of all his deposits with the bank or BD15,000 (US$39,788).

The Deposit Protection Board operates the Scheme. The Board is made up of 10 members, two of whom represent the BMA, with one of these being nominated as chairman; four representing the commercial banks; one representing each of the Ministries of Finance and National Economy, Commerce and Justice and one representing the Bahrain Chamber of Commerce and Industry.

The total annual value of the Scheme is BD25 million (US$66.3 million), although unused funds from the preceding year and the following year may also be utilised. This suggests availability, in principle, of a maximum sum of BD75 million (US$199 million). If the amount payable to depositors is greater than the actual amount available under the Scheme, all payments will be made on a pro-rata basis.

The Scheme comes fully into operation after default of a local commercial bank with participating banks bearing the cost of compensation on an equitable basis. However, consideration is being given to upgrading the Scheme whereby it will become pre-funded up to an initial amount of BD60 million (US$159 million) whilst retaining post-funded cover for the excess (up to BD75 million), although the BMA stresses that this must not be looked upon as an alternative to its own stringent banking supervision activities. Creating readily available funding would enable speed of action and consequently minimise or reduce social difficulties which could arise for depositors. Under the proposed Scheme, banks' contributions will remain directly linked to the overall size of all the deposits which they hold on any type of account.

Protection of investors using financial and investment advisory services

To protect investors against fraud and negligence, the BMA has introduced the need for the licensing, organising and supervising of all investment and financial consultancies operating in and from Bahrain and of all collective investment schemes, including mutual funds and unit trusts, that are made available to investors in and from Bahrain.

Safeguarding the banking system against credit risks

Since its establishment, the BMA has sought to provide local commercial banks with the tools to deal with banking risks in a prudent and cautious manner to ensure the security of their funds and to enable them to grow and prosper. The first step taken in this regard was the licensing of all financial institutions, which enabled the BMA to regulate and supervise their activities. But equally important has been the BMA's role in seeking cooperation from the banks in acquiring the latest analytical systems for measuring credit risk, so as to guarantee the soundness of their assets and investment portfolios.

The role of the BMA's Central Risk Unit is central to this activity. Its primary task is to monitor lending risks. Whilst all banks are obligated to measure their own credit risks they are also expected to cooperate with the BMA by providing detailed information on borrowers with exposure above a defined amount. Such information is provided by the banks as an aggregate amount. This enables the BMA to assess fully the overall financial situation of the Bahraini banking system and therefore the level of risk entailed.

Despite the undoubted effectiveness of the analysis and supervision of the risks involved, borrowers may face financial difficulties leading to excess exposure by one or more banks. Under such circumstances the BMA encourages banks to set aside adequate provisions to cover potential losses. By way of assistance, the BMA provides local commercial banks with information on the latest methods for assessing and measuring both country risks and the risks of borrowers facing payment difficulties in order to determine the level of provisioning required.

The provision of support to banks through the introduction of modern techniques in credit risk analysis, and through the supervision of their activities through inspections and the analysis of their regular returns, has proved vital over past years to the maintenance of stability and confidence in Bahrain's banking sector. As banking and finance develop and diversify, and their underlying activities become increasingly complex, so the role of the BMA and its Central Risk Unit becomes increasingly vital in ensuring Bahrain maintains its status as a well-regulated and supervised financial centre.

Safeguarding the banking system against dishonoured cheques

The BMA, under the terms of its founding law, was charged with protecting all banking operations from malpractice and irregularity. This included the increasing problem of dishonoured cheques. The BMA devised a scheme whereby information and data were collected on those who frequently issued cheques that were subsequently returned unpaid. Their names were circulated to all commercial banks in Bahrain with a request they exercise caution in any dealings with them. However, controlling this activity was prevented by the absence of any meaningful action against those responsible.

It was in 1996, following proposals by the BMA, that Legislative Decree No. 5 was promulgated. This widened the available powers against those who constantly abused cheques. Under this amendment, the BMA was able to issue rules and regulations entitled 'Regulation Relating to a Penalty System for Dishonoured Cheques', which laid down a course of action to be taken by the commercial banks and, in turn, by the BMA with effect from 1 January 1997.

The regulations were intended to specifically punish any natural or corporate person whose cheque was dishonoured due to an insufficient balance on the account on which it was drawn. The penalties imposed ranged from warnings and the publication of their names to the closure of their accounts and the halting of dealings with them by all local banks.

Since the introduction of these regulations, significant success has been achieved in reducing the number of cheques being returned. In 1995 and 1996 the percentage of

Exhibit 11.1: Returned cheques statistics, 1995-2001

Year	*No of cheques cleared*	*No of returned cheques*	*% of returned cheques*
1995	1,958,946	89,328	4.56
1996	1,926,316	85,208	4.42
1997	1,906,810	68,223	3.58
1998	1,952,318	64,935	3.33
1999	1,898,360	67,290	3.54
2000	1,944,638	63,899	3.29
2001	2,023,870	58,996	2.92
2002	2,074,000	52,982	2.55

Source: Bahrain Monetary Agency.

Exhibit 11.2: Amount of returned cheques statistics, 1995-2001 (BD)

Year cleared	*Amount of cheques*	*Amount of returned cheques*	*% of returned cheques*
1995	1,146,043,035	48,825,318	4.2
1996	1,158,453,280	46,840,509	4.0
1997	1,214,572,203	39,673,604	3.2
1998	1,305,906,708	41,040,349	3.1
1999	1,266,210,131	46,012,643	3.6
2000	1,365,976,189	43,687,093	3.2
2001	1,578,393,556	44,642,683	2.8
2002	1,810,000,000	40,130,000	2.2

Source: Bahrain Monetary Agency.

cheques returned amounted to 4.56 per cent and 4.42 per cent respectively. Between 1997 and the end of 2001 (with the exception of 1999), the level of returned cheques fell year-on-year until the percentage had reached just 2.92 per cent. In 2002 there was a further decline in the number of returned cheques of 10 per cent, from 58,996 to 52,982, on an increased number of cheques cleared totalling 2.074 million. This figure indicates an increase of 2.5 per cent from the previous year, when there had also been a rise in the number of cheques passing through the system.

The overall value in cheques returned as a percentage of the value of cheques cleared was reduced from 4.26 per cent in 1997 to 2.22 per cent in 2002.

The effectiveness of the implementation of the regulations is self-evident, not only from the reduced level of cheques being returned but also from the higher usage of cheques within the system, which indicates the increased confidence of the business community as a whole in using and accepting cheques as a means of payment. Despite the improvement in the figures, the BMA wants to see a further drop in both the number and value of cheques being dishonoured.

12
International role

Introduction

Bahrain is very much part of the international environment and, in this increasingly small world, recognises the need to work together with other governments and international bodies across the globe. As an international financial centre, the Kingdom is part of a worldwide network of financial institutions and regulatory authorities with whose principles, policies, rules and regulations the BMA recognises the need to integrate. To achieve this, Bahrain has become a member of and closely associated with many international and regional organisations, including those that have an impact on the financial sector. Both the Government and the BMA have nurtured these relationships since the time the country became a fully independent state. As the region's leading international financial centre such associations help the BMA's effectiveness as regulator and supervisor, thereby ensuring Bahrain becomes an increasingly attractive destination for banks and financial institutions.

Alongside the undoubted benefits that membership of such entities confers, there are obligations to be met such as ensuring full compliance with all international agreements. The BMA has been diligent in its efforts to ensure such compliance and maintains a dialogue with its fellow members to their mutual benefit. The BMA is also actively involved in promoting the growing Islamic financial movement, and not just in those countries where Islam is the predominant religion but also elsewhere in countries where significant, albeit minority, Muslim populations are to be found.

International Monetary Fund (IMF)

In September 1972, Bahrain became a member of the IMF with a membership quota of SDR10 million (SDR = Special Drawing Rights), which was assigned, like that of every member of the IMF, according to the country's national income, monetary reserves, balance of trade and other economic indicators. Subsequently, the quota has been increased on a number of occasions in line with general reviews undertaken by the IMF, such that today Bahrain's quota is SDR135 million, or about 0.06 per cent of total SDRs in issue, SDR212.7 billion. This quota determines, in the main, a member's voting power which is, in the case of Bahrain, 1,600 votes or 0.07 per cent of the current total.

Bahrain's association with the IMF has continued for many years with the Fund undertaking macroeconomic reviews of Bahrain (Article IV Consultation) every 18 months. Such reviews analyse the national economy, the financial sector and their interrelated policies and, on completion, result in the provision of detailed reports and recommendations.

The BMA continuously works to maintain the increasingly stringent global standards applicable to financial institutions and therefore looks to the IMF for guidance in this regard. Bahrain will also be participating in the IMF's Financial Stability Assessment Programme which focuses specifically on structural issues in the financial sector. Bahrain was rewarded with a high compliance ratio with Basel Committee core principles on the last occasion supervision was addressed by the IMF in 2000.

The World Bank

At the same time as becoming a member of the IMF in September 1972, Bahrain gained membership of the International Bank for Reconstruction and Development (IBRD or World Bank). The Fund and the Bank are sister organisations, although to be able to be a member of the World Bank only members of the IMF are considered.

As a member of the GCC, Bahrain has been a beneficiary of the World Bank's Technical Cooperation Programme with the GCC which, in earlier years, provided support to the Government in the development of infrastructure, industrial development and economic planning. Today, the World Bank is available to cooperate with the government in the development of macroeconomic and sectoral policies, and in particular with human resource development, environmental protection and the ongoing promotion of the private sector, but has so far not been called upon to assist in any specific manner.

In the 1980s, Bahrain drew on the resources of a member of The World Bank Group, the International Finance Corporation (IFC), to undertake a comprehensive feasibility study, which led over time to the founding of the Bahrain Stock Exchange.

The World Trade Organisation (WTO)

Bahrain officially became a member of the General Agreement on Tariffs and Trade in December 1993 and subsequently was a signatory to the Marrakech Protocol on the conclusion of the Uruguay Round, thereby becoming a founder member of the WTO when it came into being in January 1995. Prior to this, in 1994, Bahrain had presented its insurance sector commitments in preparation for membership.

The Kingdom regards membership of the WTO as vital to its developmental strategy and following accession submitted further schedules of commitments in the area of services. Two years later, in 1997, it participated in the financial services negotiations, submitting a schedule of banking sector and Stock Exchange commitments, which were subsequently updated in the first half of 2003.

Under the terms of WTO membership each country must undergo a regular Trade Policy Review, which in the case of Bahrain takes place every six years. Bahrain successfully completed such a review in October 2000, receiving accolades from the chairman and members of the review committee for the progress made in developing the national economy and for meeting its agreed commitments.

Recognising the importance of world markets and inward investment, Bahrain has progressively opened its economy and sought to find a competitive edge internationally, firmly believing that the new global economy under the mechanism of the WTO allied to the Kingdom's openness provide the country with the best opportunity for further economic success.

The Arab Monetary Fund (AMF)

The AMF is a regional financial institution headquartered in Abu Dhabi in the United Arab Emirates whose membership is open to all members of the Arab League. Bahrain became a founder member of the AMF in November 1976, prior to commencement of its operations in 1977, with a subscription to its capital at that time equal to 80 shares with a value of 4 million Arab dinars. Since that time, the capital of the AMF has been increased from 268 million Arab dinars to 600 million Arab dinars and Bahrain's membership subscription has increased to 9 million Arab dinars.

Integral to the AMF is also the Secretariat of the Council of Governors of Central Banks and Monetary Agencies, in which body the BMA is well-represented. Also, the AMF cooperates closely with the Arab Trade Financing Programme, to which Bahrain, through the BMA, is a subscriber, and whose role is the promotion of trade between Arab countries through the provision of lines of credit available through approved national agencies which, in the case of Bahrain, includes the Bahrain Development Bank, National Bank of Bahrain and the Arab Banking Corporation.

The Islamic Development Bank (IDB)

The IDB is an international financial institution, headquartered in Jeddah, Saudi Arabia. The Bank formally opened in Shawal 1395 (October 1975) with an authorised capital of 2 billion Islamic dinars (one Islamic dinar (ID) is equivalent to one SDR) and today has 54 members, all of whom are, by definition, members of the Organisation of Islamic Conferences (OIC). The authorised capital of the IDB was revised in July 1992 to 6 million Islamic dinars with Bahrain's subscription to the capital being ID7 million or 0.17 per cent of the total paid-up.

The BMA has worked closely with the IDB to develop Islamic financial markets. Specifically, cooperation has included such entities as the International Islamic Financial Market (IIFM), the International Islamic Rating Agency (IIRA), which was an IDB initiative, and the Liquidity Management Centre (LMC) in which the IDB is a founder shareholder along with Bahrain and a number of other states (see Chapter 6 for further details).

A further initiative is the IDB Infrastructure Fund LP, the first private sector investment vehicle to focus on infrastructure development in the Islamic world. The fund, which has an equity capital of US$1 billion and a complementary finance facility of US$500 million, has been set up in Bahrain, where the Fund's Policy Management Committee also resides, and provides the opportunity for governments and private investors to participate in the funding of a diversified group of infrastructure projects, wherever possible according to Islamic criteria. A secondary aim of the Fund is to encourage the development of national and regional capital markets through the public listing of those companies in which the fund invests.

Bahrain is also a member in the fledgling Islamic Corporation for the Development of the Private Sector (ICD), which is also part of the IDB Group. ICD has an authorised capital of US$1 billion, of which half is paid-up. The intention of the ICD is to provide Islamic financing for private sector projects, to assist the private sector in OIC member countries to mobilise financial resources and to offer member countries a wide range of consultancy services to enhance their private sectors.

The Cooperation Council of the Arab States of the Gulf (GCC)

The GCC, better known as the Gulf Cooperation Council, was formed in 1981 by the six Arab states bordering the Arabian Gulf, namely Bahrain, Kuwait, Oman, Qatar, Saudi Arabia and the United Arab Emirates, with the specific aim of establishing a framework of close cooperation between member states in order to effect coordination, integration and interconnection between them and especially, but not solely, in the fields of economy, finance, trade, customs, tourism, legislation and administration.

Since the beginning of the twenty-first century, specific attention has been given by the GCC to creating an environment conducive to the establishment of a common market and monetary and economic union. As a result, full customs union was attained by 2003 and full monetary union, with a single currency, is planned for the beginning of 2010 or possibly 2007. Already, Bahrain has initiated moves to reduce customs duties in line with customs union proposals and, in December 2001, took the first step towards a single currency by removing the dinar's linkage with the SDR and tying it to the US dollar, something that all six states have now done.

The BMA's cooperation with others to develop the banking sector in the GCC goes back more than two decades, when it began to work together with other GCC central banks and monetary agencies in developing a mechanism for unifying the exchange rates of the GCC currencies. Efforts were also made towards the establishment of simple procedures for credit facilities among the GCC central banks and monetary agencies. The primary purpose of these procedures was to enable the relevant central banks and monetary agencies to ensure an easy flow of funds to cover their short-term requirements without the need to resort to drawing down their reserves or borrowing from external markets.

Since the early 1980s, through the collective efforts of the GCC Governors' Committee, a number of proposals have been put forward concerning cooperation between the GCC central banks and monetary agencies in connection with the execution of Article 22 of the GCC Economic Agreement. These proposals have sought the development of the financial relationship between GCC members and the establishment of a unified Gulf currency. Other areas covered by the GCC Governors' Committee have included:

- local credit policy;
- control and supervision of the banking sector;
- exchange rate policies;
- establishment of a unified clearing system;
- introduction of a Gulf-wide ATM network;
- relationships with other financial centres; and
- issues relating to banking training within the GCC.

The BMA has participated in all the meetings of the GCC Central Bank Governors' Committee and has been integral to improving cooperation between the central banks for the purpose of achieving the goals of the GCC Economic Agreement. Many of the Agency's proposals, including the unified exchange rate system, were accepted by the Committee, whose members' combined activities have been wholly integral to financial and economic progress within the GCC. The BMA has also played a vital role in formulating and developing the financial situation and practices of GCC banks.

The Basel Committee on Banking Supervision

The Basel Committee, established in 1974 by the Central Bank Governors of the Group of Ten (G10) countries, is a committee of central banks and bank supervisors and regulators from major industrialised countries that meets at the Bank for International Settlements (BIS) in Basel. The Committee's primary role is to formulate broad advisory standards and guidelines with global applicability and recommend statements of best practice for the banking sector. It is expected that individual authorities will take steps to implement them through detailed arrangements, statutory or otherwise, which are best suited to their own national systems. Bahrain is not a member of the Basel Committee but does seek convergence with its recommendations, in particular the framework for banks' capital adequacy and the basic principles for effective banking supervision.

As of June 2003 the BMA was also addressing the new Basel proposals, known as Basel II, which seek to improve materially the basis for capital regulation in the banking sector by placing more emphasis on banks' own internal assessments of capital requirements, enhanced supervisory review, and market discipline. Once the consultative process has been completed, in which the BMA is playing a role, Basel II is expected to be introduced as the new advisory standards and guidelines and the BMA is expected to seek broad compliance with them by all banks in Bahrain.

To maintain its position at the forefront of the regulatory and supervisory field, the BMA participates also in an International Conference of Banking Supervisors which the Basel Committee organises every two years, as well as in other relevant international fora such as the Offshore Group of Banking Supervisors.

The Bank for International Settlements (BIS)

The BIS is the oldest international financial institution, having been formed in 1930 to deal with reparation payments imposed by the Treaty of Versailles at the end of World War I. The BIS has evolved to become increasingly involved in the promotion of cooperation between central banks worldwide. Today, the BIS essentially provides a forum for central bank cooperation, conducts research contributing to monetary and financial stability and performs traditional banking functions on behalf of central banks and international organisations. It is able also to provide or organise funding in support of the international monetary system as and when needed. The BIS hosts the secretariats of the Financial Stability Forum (FSF), the International Association of Deposit Insurers (IADI), and the International Association of Insurance Supervisors (IAIS). It also operates the Financial Stability Institute (FSI) jointly with the Basel Committee on Banking Supervision. The BMA is not a member of the BIS but does maintain a financial relationship with it. Bahrain may seek membership in the future.

International Association of Insurance Supervisors (IAIS)

The BMA, as the single regulator for the whole of Bahrain's financial sector, with responsibility therefore for the insurance sector, became a member of the IAIS in 2002. Having been formed in 1994, the organisation represents insurance supervisory authorities in over 100 jurisdictions with the basic aim of developing international supervisory standards. More specifically, the IAIS fills a role in promoting cooperation among insurance regulators, setting international standards for insurance supervision, providing training for members, and coordinating work with regulators in other financial sectors and with financial institutions.

In addition, the IAIS has also encouraged the membership of insurance professionals as observer members. To date, over 60 industry and professional associations, insurance and reinsurance companies, consultants and international financial institutions have joined. Since joining the IAIS, the BMA has initiated an analysis to enable identification of those areas of regulation and supervision which need to be brought further into line with IAIS core principles. These principles cover such areas as licensing and changes in control, corporate governance and internal controls, prudential rules, market conduct and monitoring, and on-site inspection.

The International Organisation of Securities Commissions (IOSCO)

The Bahrain Stock Exchange (BSE) is an ordinary member of IOSCO and is represented on the Organisation's Emerging Markets Committee. In pursuing its activities, in recent years the BSE has sought to comply with the recommendations of IOSCO, a role which has now passed to the BMA, which continues to look at improving its regulatory and supervisory activities so as to be fully in accordance with best international practice.

The Financial Action Task Force on Money Laundering (FATF)

The FATF is an intergovernmental body established by the G7 countries in 1989 as a result of increasing concerns about international money laundering. The role of the FATF is to develop and promote policies to combat money laundering on both national and international levels.

The FATF monitors the progress of members in implementing anti-money laundering measures, reviews money laundering techniques and counter-measures and promotes the adoption of anti-money laundering measures worldwide.

A major document prepared by the FATF, with which the BMA seeks full compliance, is 'The 40 Recommendations on Money Laundering', which sets out the measures which the Task Force has agreed to implement and which all countries are encouraged to adopt. These measures were originally drawn up in 1990, were revised in 1996 and were again updated in 2003. They are drawn to the attention of central banks and financial institutions on a regular basis to seek to ensure continued compliance.

Following the events of 11 September 2001, the FATF also took action in regard to the funding of terrorism and, in January 2002, introduced 'Special Recommendations on Terrorist Financing'. There are eight recommendations setting out a framework to enable the detection, prevention and suppression of the financing of terrorism and terrorist acts.

Bahrain is not a direct member of FATF, indeed only 29 countries are, but is so through its membership of the GCC, which does participate. Bahrain does work actively, however, to seek to comply fully with the recommendations made, which are equally as applicable to the Kingdom's insurance sector and the BSE as to the country's banking and financial community.

Participation in these international bodies by the Government or the BMA provides direct access to the best possible advice and assistance on economic and financial matters; enables the BMA to fulfil a role in defining the parameters within which the global banking community, and therefore Bahrain's international financial centre, might operate; and ensures the banks and financial institutions can operate in a regulatory and supervisory environment akin to that in other major financial centres around the world. Such an environment inspires confidence among the international financial community, thereby ensuring Bahrain can maintain its status as the location of choice for those seeking a presence in the Middle East and also as the leading financial capital of the region.

13
The human resource and wider roles of the BMA

Human resource development in Bahrain

The government of Bahrain has consistently recognised that the country's primary asset is its people and that they are wholly integral to the successful growth of the country's economy in the years to come. As a result the full development of the Kingdom's human resources has been a primary aim, resulting early in the 1990s in the taking of the initiative to develop and introduce a new human resource development strategy.

Over the ensuing years clear evidence of the success of the strategy can be seen on the ground, especially in the growth of educational and training establishments, including the Bahrain Institute of Banking and Finance, and the increasing numbers of Bahrainis not only taking their rightful place in gainful employment but also rising to senior positions in both government and the private sector, including in banking and finance. Equally importantly, the success of the policies introduced has received international recognition in the 14th Report of the UNDP's Human Development Index, 2002, in which Bahrain has successfully retained its position of 37th among the 175 countries covered for the third year running and, especially gratifying, first among all Arab States.

Such an achievement is very much a direct result of national political and economic stability, the availability of an appropriate infrastructure in the country and the existence of clearly defined pro-active human resource development policies. The standards set undoubtedly provide a daunting challenge for the coming generation but nevertheless make Bahrain an attractive location for foreign investment and confirm that

Exhibit 13.1: Employment in the banking and financial sectors, 2000-02

	2000			*2001*			*2002*		
Sectors	*Bahraini*	*Non-Bahraini*	*Total*	*Bahraini*	*Non-Bahraini*	*Total*	*Bahraini*	*Non-Bahraini*	*Total*
Banking sector									
Commercial banks	2,015	290	2,305	1,857	265	2,122	1,919	232	2,151
OBUs	996	482	1,478	1,097	512	1,609	1,118	567	1,685
Investment banks	649	278	927	707	275	982	764	278	1,042
Representative offices	32	54	86	27	54	81	24	43	67
Total	**3,692**	**1,104**	**4,796**	**3,688**	**1,106**	**4,794**	**3,825**	**1,120**	**4,945**
Financial sector									
Insurance	-	-	-	-	-	-	484	260	744
Other	190	245	435	186	252	438	243	283	526
Grand total	**3,882**	**1,349**	**5,231**	**3,874**	**1,358**	**5,232**	**4,552**	**1,663**	**6,215**

Sources: Bahrain Monetary Agency *Annual Report 2001* and BMA Press Release, March 2003.

Bahrain is a suitable place for international businesses and financial institutions to establish a presence.

The BMA and training

The BMA has been the driving force behind employee education and training in the banking and financial sector since the 1970s. The employment of Bahrainis in the banking and finance sector, which is the largest single employer in Bahrain, has been one of the most important aims of the BMA. Equally important has been the level of education and training made available for employees in the sector to enhance their knowledge and expertise and, over time, their experience, so to ensure their increasingly significant contribution in the years to come.

Employment in the banking and finance industry increased in 2002 to 6,215, a rise of 18.8 per cent over the previous year-end. Of the total, Bahraini workers numbered 4,552, or 73 per cent, of which 3,079 were men and 1,473 were women. On a sectoral basis, full commercial banks employed 2,151 people (1,919 or 89 per cent being Bahrainis); OBUs employed 1,685 (1,118 Bahrainis); investment banks 1,042 (764); representative offices 67

(24); and non-bank financial entities 1,270 (727), of which figure the insurance sector was the largest employer with a total of 744, of whom 484 were Bahrainis.

Specific Council for Vocational Training (Banking Sector) - SCVT

Initially the BMA provided training courses at banks which had available facilities. Subsequently, the Bankers' Training Centre (BTC) was established, which ultimately became the Bahrain Institute of Banking and Finance (BIBF), to provide professional training exclusively for Bahrainis employed in the banking and financial sector. The intention of the BTC was to be active in organising training and educational courses in specialised banking fields thereby to improve the capabilities, performance and efficiency of financial sector employees so integral to the government's policies of enhancing national employment whilst ensuring economic diversification.

At the outset, the BTC was placed under the direct supervision of the SCVT, which is a government body charged with providing vocational training for Bahrainis. The SCVT is an integral element of the Higher Council for Vocational Training, formed by Amiri Decree with the primary aim of ensuring relevant vocational training was available for Bahraini nationals to help them improve their skills and gain employment.

The Chairman of the SCVT is the Governor of the BMA, who is supported by a number of senior members of the banking, Islamic banking, insurance and finance industries and by a representative of the University of Bahrain. Today, the SCVT provides strategic direction to the BIBF, oversees its budget and advises on and confirms its three-year strategic plan. The SCVT meets the BIBF quarterly to review progress and to make any necessary amendments to the plan and to the programmes being offered in the light of developments in the sectors covered by the BIBF's activities.

As both the international financial centre and the BTC, and later the BIBF, have grown so too have there been rapid technological advances and growing competition between the banks and financial institutions in Bahrain. The BMA, the SCVT and the BIBF have sought constantly to ensure that the level of vocational training available grows commensurately to the needs of the banking and financial sector and to the overall benefit of Bahrain and its people.

Throughout the development of the BTC and the BIBF, the BMA has played a pivotal role, especially through the Management Services Directorate, in ensuring the nature and level of training and education being provided is relevant to the needs of the day. Thus the BMA has maintained close ties with the training directors and managers in the banking sector and, as it becomes increasingly responsible for the insurance sector and the Bahrain Stock Exchange (BSE), is seeking relationships with the people responsible for training in those sectors as well. As a result, the BMA undertakes studies and research to ascertain the level of training in the banking and financial sector and also develops and circulates questionnaires that aim to ascertain the training needs of banks and financial institutions on an ongoing basis.

In addition, the BMA recognises the importance of training to enhance the quality of its own staff, which it deems essential to its ability to function effectively as a central monetary authority in a rapidly changing banking and financial environment. Throughout their employment with the BMA, staff are evaluated for training on management, technical and behavioural bases and are provided with relevant training opportunities both in Bahrain and outside. Over the years, the BMA has sent a number of staff on courses abroad to locations including The World Bank, the Bank of England, Banque du Liban, the Saudi Arabian Monetary Agency and the Arab Centre for Research and Crime Studies. In Bahrain, participants attended courses at the BIBF, whilst others participated in courses, seminars and workshops presented by a range of organisations. As appropriate, the BMA also considers the possibility of sending employees to university to further pursue their studies.

Regular contact is maintained with other monetary authorities around the world, such as those in Hong Kong and Singapore, the Banque de France and the Bank of England. Whilst such contacts address all aspects of central banking, training is also an integral element.

Human Resource Development Fund (HRDF)

The HRDF was developed by the BMA with the support of the Government, which provided an initial investment of BD500,000, and aims to 'bridge specific skills gaps in the prevailing training environment and to finance specific training programmes of a professional and technical nature'. To these ends, it is anticipated some 25 training courses will be provided annually.

Within the BMA a Talent Pool Task Force has been formed to develop reviews and proposals for the Fund and which has been mandated to study means of further enhancing human resources in the financial sector. As part of its role, the Task Force has launched a number of scholarship and internship programmes for Bahrainis.

The Bahrain Institute of Banking and Finance (BIBF)

The BIBF started life as The Bahrain Bankers' Training Centre in March 1981. In March 1989, it was renamed, along with the official opening of new, purpose-built premises in Juffair by HH the Prime Minister, Shaikh Khalifa bin Salman Al Khalifa, and operates under the guidance of the SCVT. The primary mission of the BIBF is to provide contemporary training and education in the areas of management, information technology, banking, insurance and finance to Bahraini officers and staff of institutions in the banking, financial and insurance sectors.

The Institute is funded by a 1 per cent levy on the annual payrolls of banks and insurance companies in Bahrain. The levy covers the costs for employees of these institutions to attend the Institute. However, Bahrainis from non-levy-paying organisations and participants from other institutions within the GCC States and the wider region may also attend but on a fee-paying basis.

Two years after it opened, the BIBF introduced a Banking Studies Diploma Programme. Participants could study for a local banking qualification or the Diploma of the Chartered Institute of Bankers in the United Kingdom, for which the Institute is a recognised examination centre. Since inception of the Banking Studies Diploma

Exhibit 13.2: BIBF participant days, 2002

	Public offerings	*Special offerings*	*Externals*	*Professional qualifications*	*Total*
Accounting and finance	1,824	2,786	0	2,374	6,984
Financial services	2,692	7,295	858	4,660	15,505
Information technology	2,578	724	0	208	3,510
Insurance	2,112	7,508	153	108	9,881
Islamic banking and finance	136	1,330	287	854	2,607
Leadership and management	2,961	961	271	2,916	7,109
Total	**12,303**	**20,604**	**1,569**	**11,120**	**45,596**

Source: Bahrain Institute of Banking and Finance.

Programme, nearly 5,000 students have enrolled, mainly for the local qualification, of which 427 have graduated at intermediate level and 231 at advanced level.

In September 1986 the Department of Insurance Studies was established within the Institute to provide the specific training and development needs of the local insurance industry. More than 1,400 attendees have participated in insurance-related courses with a further 1,300 insurance industry personnel having joined other institute courses.

The Institute is divided into six learning centres and the courses offered according to the 2002 courses programme included:

- *Accounting and finance.* This centre was to provide 25 courses during 2002 including basic business and study skills, core accounting (financial and management), financial analysis, financial management, finance and budgeting for the non-financial manager, calculations and statistics and auditing;
- *Financial services* holds 32 courses during the year, which include domestic banking, treasury, credit and credit analysis, international banking and capital markets;
- *Information technology* holds 33 courses covering spreadsheets, word-processing, desktop publishing, database development and graphics;
- *Insurance studies* covers general, property, motor, marine and aviation, accident and life and health insurance through the provision of 16 courses leading to an Insurance Diploma, which is available in English or Arabic, and an Advanced Diploma, which is available only in English.
- *Islamic banking and finance* addresses the *Shari'a*, banking, accounting, financial analysis and management in an Islamic environment through a total of 11 courses; and
- *Leadership and management courses* include management skills, communications, professional productivity, personnel development, leadership and management and executive training and development through 29 courses at four levels – administrative, junior management, middle management and executive management.

In addition to these 146 courses, the BIBF prepares and designs special courses for client banks and financial institutions in Bahrain, around the Gulf and sometimes other locations worldwide.

As a provider of quality training, the Institute has established links with a number of professional and academic bodies. The BIBF is an accredited examination centre for many of these. They include four from the United Kingdom (the first four listed below) and five from the United States:

- Chartered Institute of Bankers;
- Chartered Insurance Institute (whose course materials the BIBF has had officially translated into Arabic);
- Chartered Institute of Management Accounting;
- Association of Certified Chartered Accountants;
- American Institute of Property Insurers;
- International Securities Market Association;
- DePaul University in Chicago;
- Bentley College near Boston; and
- Becker CPA Review in California.

The associations with DePaul and Bentley lead on to an MBA and Bachelor's Degree in Business Management respectively, with courses leading up to both qualifications being held in Bahrain at the BIBF.

The BIBF can boast in excess of 300 professionally qualified graduates of the UK and US institutes and associations mentioned, especially those providing banking, insurance and accountancy qualifications.

A Gulf Executive Development Programme has also been available for some years in association with the Darden Graduate School of Business at the University of Virginia. As of mid-2002 there were 115 graduates of this programme, a number set to grow to nearer 150 by the end of the current, fourth, programme.

Affiliations are also maintained with a number of entities that offer seminars and workshops, including:

- International Monetary Fund;
- World Bank;
- Federal Reserve Bank of New York;
- Federal Insurance Organization of the United States of America;
- Securities Exchange Commission;
- PricewaterhouseCoopers;

- Islamic Development Bank; and
- Accounting and Auditing Organization for Islamic Financial Institutions (AAOIFI).

Through such affiliations, the Institute has enabled the exchange of ideas and technical information leading to the support and development of its own training programmes. As a result, the BIBF has become a pre-eminent centre for training and education in banking and finance, drawing attendees not only from the other Gulf States but also from the wider region.

In recent years, the growth in interest in Islamic banking and finance has led to the BIBF introducing the Advanced Islamic Banking Diploma for those wishing to pursue a career in the sector. Furthermore, the requirement that all brokers involved with the BSE must hold at least the Investment Representative Programme Certificate before they are allowed to trade has resulted in the introduction by the BIBF of courses leading to this qualification.

In the pursuit of creating professional bankers from amongst the indigenous population who are well-able to handle the latest developments in international banking, attention is also given by the BIBF to e-commerce, e-banking and e-technology in general but especially as it applies to banking, finance and insurance.

The overall success of the Institute in raising the qualifications of banking, finance and insurance staff throughout the Middle East, but especially in Bahrain itself, is best reflected in the figures to the end of the second quarter of 2002, by when over 46,000 participants had attended courses, approximately 85 per cent of whom had been Bahrainis or Gulf nationals. Most importantly, the BIBF's success to date provides a firm platform on which to build for the long-term future to ensure continued growth and professionalism of Bahrain's banking and financial sector.

Centre for Research in Islamic Banking and Finance (CRIBF)

A major challenge on the road to enhancing the reputation of Bahrain as a centre of excellence in Islamic banking, finance and insurance is the development of career training programmes for the sector. With this in mind, the BMA is actively pursuing the creation of the CRIBF in Bahrain as a world-class Islamic financial training, education and research centre. When opened the Centre will:

NBB banking hall

- offer degree programmes to create a new generation of professionally and technically qualified Islamic bankers and other professionals for the industry;
- undertake market-driven Islamic financial research – practical aspects of Islamic banking, rather than theory, such as studies on management systems, divergence of *Shari'a* judgements and the regulation of Islamic banks; and
- stimulate product innovation to expand consumer choice and provide profitable trading opportunities for Islamic financial institutions.

The Bankers' Society of Bahrain

Established in 1979 by Ministerial Decree, at a time when the number of offshore banking units was growing rapidly, this is the professional association of banks licensed in Bahrain. Membership of the Society is not compulsory but at the end of the first quarter of 2002 the number of members totalled 95.

The Society represents the interests of all licensed banks in Bahrain, including commercial, offshore and investment banks, Islamic banks and representative offices. It also has a very close working relationship with the BMA, the Ministry of Finance and National Economy and other government agencies with whom it discusses issues such as banking policy, control and regulation. The Society also actively promotes Bahrain as an international financial centre. The Society is run by an elected executive committee comprising 12 chief executives of financial institutions licensed in Bahrain.

The defined objectives of the Society are:

- representation of the interests of the banking community in Bahrain both within the Kingdom and abroad;
- promotion of Bahrain as an international financial centre of excellence;
- liaison with the highest levels of government on all aspects of banking regulation and policy which affect the banking sector;
- provision of assistance in the development of plans, proposals and strategies for the advancement of the banking sector in Bahrain;
- provision of a forum for member banks to meet and hold open discussions;
- participation in and support of conferences and seminars, as well as hosting official overseas representations and visiting senior bankers;
- formation of committees and sub-committees to examine specific issues of importance, especially those affecting banking and finance in Bahrain; and
- supporting professional training and development in the banking sector through the BIBF.

Since its formation, the Society has grown from strength to strength as a result of both the strong support of member banks and the high level of cooperation with the BMA. As evidence of this synergy, the executive committee of the Society meets regularly with HE the Governor of the BMA at consultative meetings. Joint sub-committees, comprising members of the Society and the BMA, are frequently formed to discuss matters of importance to the banking sector and to implement projects and policies essential to the sector's future development. All circulars issued by the BMA are brought to the attention of, and are consulted upon by, the banking community through the Society. Also, the Society, through its senior members, is very closely involved with the SCVT and the BIBF so as to ensure the continued employability and availability of Bahrainis who are suitably prepared and qualified to enter and make a career of banking and finance.

Such ongoing communication, cooperation and consultation, allied to an excellent level of support provided by the Government of Bahrain, as well as the introduction of the highest regulatory standards, have been major contributory factors in the expansion of banking and integral to ensuring the strength of Bahrain as a prime location for banking and financial activities whilst providing the necessary confidence to ensure the sector's continued success and growth over the coming decades.

Bahrain Insurance Association (BIA)

The BIA received its Charter in September 1993 by Ministerial Order. Membership is open to all insurance companies registered in Bahrain, be they onshore or offshore, and as of mid-2002 the Association had 18 members, these being national local companies, branches of foreign companies, reinsurance companies and brokers, who are mainly the international brokers present in Bahrain. No offshore companies numbered among the 18.

The Association perceives its role as that of the focal point for the insurance industry in Bahrain and as a catalyst between the companies, the authorities and the media, in fulfilment of which it has maintained a close relationship in the past with the Ministry of Commerce and Industry, as the former regulatory authority for the insurance sector, and with the BMA today. An indication of the Association's proximity with the authorities has been its involvement in closely examining and providing feedback on the new draft legislation presently under consideration for upgrading the regulatory environment in Bahrain.

The Association's primary objectives are to:

- provide a common platform for all insurance companies operating in Bahrain;
- increase awareness of the public in all insurance-related matters;
- liaise and interact with government bodies in regard to legislation and other matters of mutual interest;
- provide training to increase the level of professionalism in the industry;
- promote Bahrain as an international insurance centre;

- standardise the underwriting and claims procedures followed by the market; and
- compile and publish statistical data on premiums and claims related to the local insurance market.

To enable performance of these objectives, the management of the Association has been vested in a Board of Directors, comprising nine senior representatives of the insurance industry in Bahrain, five of whom have specific responsibilities for technical and legal affairs, public relations, training, research and development and association services. Under the Board, four technical committees have been established specific to defined classes of insurance, namely: fire, engineering and general accident; life and medical; motor; and marine and aviation.

The primary activities pursued by the Association include dialogue with government authorities; ensuring the recruitment and training of Bahraini nationals in association with the BIBF and the BTI; the presentation of seminars and workshops; the devising of guide rates and drafting of policies and clauses for the market; preparing statistical reports; and arranging reinsurance cover for insurance perils where these are peculiar to the Bahrain market.

Of specific importance during 2001 and 2002, has been the Association's close involvement in examining from a professional perspective the draft resolutions for further regulation of the insurance industry. The new regulations foresee marked developments in the sector with more stringent capital requirements, solvency margins and reserve requirements, as well as in such areas as the definition of different categories of licence, increased supervision and a separation between consultants, brokers and actuarial activities. In all these regards, the Association is directly involved in bringing together the combined experience, expertise and knowledge of representatives of both local and international insurance companies in Bahrain and, wherever necessary, drawing on the opinions of the legal profession especially in regard to the impact of the national Civil Code on the new draft regulations.

In the 18 months leading up to mid-2003 the BIA has also been highly active in looking to the future of the insurance industry in Bahrain from a number of practical standpoints. These have included:

- the formation of a joint task force with the BMA to share knowledge and information which will lead to further promotion of the insurance industry within the context of Bahrain's position as the leading financial centre in the region;

- the provision of research in seeking solutions to the needs of the insurance industry in Bahrain in regard to the introduction of medical insurance for expatriates and terrorism-related insurance risks;
- working closely with the BIBF to ensure the availability of appropriately designed courses at the Insurance Learning Centre and the possibility of sending management-calibre Bahraini students to the London Guildhall University to participate in a full-time residential programme leading to the examinations of The Chartered Insurance Institute;
- liaising with the local traffic authorities and the BMA with the objective of introducing more appropriate motor ratings linked to a traffic points system which would aim to encourage safer driving; and
- examining new insurance opportunities for implementation in Bahrain.

As with the Bankers' Society, the Insurance Association also maintains a close association with the SCVT, on which the insurance industry is represented, and with the BIBF, where it has a seat on the Insurance Training Committee, in ensuring the professional diplomas and certificates being offered are beneficial to those seeking to make a career in the insurance industry. The BIA is also a board member of the General Arab Insurance Federation and the GCC Insurance Coordination Commission and, in general terms, is the collective face of the Bahrain insurance industry outside the country at all conventions, meetings and conferences.

The coming few years will be of special importance to Bahrain's insurance industry as the new regulations come into force and the country seeks to expand its role in the insurance sector through the development of a captive insurance sector for both regional and international companies. The role of the Association in ensuring the implementation of the proposed regulations will be vital, as will the need to assist the BMA in ensuring compliance, at least in part by continuing to seek to raise professional standards and thereby the enhanced reputation of Bahrain as a centre for international insurance activities.

14

The future of Bahrain as the financial capital of the Middle East

A rapidly changing environment

For some years now, the banking sector worldwide has been growing apace. The banks and financial institutions of the Middle East, and specifically those in Bahrain's international financial centre, have been working hard to keep pace with developments and especially those which impinge directly on their ability to sustain their levels of business and service in an increasingly competitive environment, where customers are ever more demanding.

In the recent past, the pace of such change in the banking sector has been exceedingly rapid. Globalisation, deregulation, enhanced competition and rapid changes in information technology have all had a major impact. The formation and growth of the financial conglomerate, handling every aspect of banking and finance from taking deposits through to the provision of insurance products, investment management and project finance, have also had an impact, even though they have not always lived up to expectations, resulting in divestments and the consolidation of core businesses.

Integral to these events has been the introduction of many new products, the development of new techniques for managing risk and the introduction of increasingly complex services. All of these have had a huge effect on the thinking of banking leaders and of those whose role it is to regulate and supervise banking and financial activities, hence the increasing prevalence of single financial regulatory authorities with the ability to oversee developments and practices across the financial spectrum.

Such authorities, be they central banks or monetary or financial services authori-

Bahrain Financial Harbour – an artist's impression

ties, in seeking to ensure proper control and oversight find it necessary to continuously examine every area of their activities. But this could not be done in isolation given the global nature of the industry, and so international cooperation has become the norm today and in this the BMA, as the single regulatory authority for Bahrain's financial centre, is very much a participant.

As the overseer of an international financial centre comprising almost 350 local and international banks, financial institutions and insurance companies, operating according to either or both conventional and Islamic principles, the BMA has been very much at the forefront of the continuing development of applicable regulatory policies and principles, whilst also ensuring that all those businesses for which it is the responsible authority pursue their activities fully in accord with the highest international standards of best practice and corporate governance.

But Bahrain is not an isolated location with a monetary authority overseeing a group of banks and financial institutions that have simply been licensed to operate in the country. The international financial centre is very much part of the global financial industry and as such must be regulated according to accepted international norms. It is thus the case that the BMA, by definition, must liaise closely with regulatory authorities worldwide whilst recognising the need to continue to pursue policies that ensure full compliance with the recommendations of such bodies as the International Monetary Fund (IMF), the Basel Committee, the Financial Action Task Force on Money Laundering (FATF) and, in the Islamic sector, the Accounting and Auditing Organization of Islamic Financial Institutions (AAOIFI).

In overseeing Bahrain's financial centre, the BMA is always fully cognisant of the fact that to maintain the country's leading role in the Middle East it constantly needs to ensure its highly deserved reputation as a well-ordered and well-regulated environment. It recognises also that sound regulation and supervision have created a healthy financial situation and a stable environment, permitting steady growth and development of Bahrain's economy, of which the financial sector has become such an important part. Such regulation necessitates the application of the latest techniques in supervision by the fully trained and professional staff of the BMA and constant interaction with its peers across the world.

The evolution of financial services

As mentioned, a major recent trend in financial services has been the formation of conglomerates combining cross-sectoral banking and financial services. Integral to the growth of such substantial entities has been the ability to offer a fully comprehensive range of products and services in a cost-effective manner to a broad base of customers. Whilst these entities may not always have proved to be very successful in an international context, the concept has yet to become generally available within Bahrain or the wider GCC.

A primary reason for such slow progress in the region is the limited size of many Gulf banks and financial institutions, many of which have very small capital bases, and a widespread lack of close interrelationships between banks and their peers in other areas of the financial community, due in large part to the private or relatively closed ownership of many of them. By way of example, only during 2002 did the GCC-wide electronic banking network, GCCNet, come fully into operation and banks from one GCC state begin to establish presences in other GCC states mainly, it has to be said, in Bahrain. It is thus self-evident that many local and regional financial institutions have a long way to go to attain the level of sophistication of much of their international competition and that to grow and prosper will necessitate enhanced cross-border activity, initially within the GCC but over time to the wider Middle East and ultimately worldwide.

Achievement of this as small, single entities seems unlikely. It is therefore perceived that the financial services sector in the Middle East, and particularly within the GCC, will need many mergers and acquisitions to take place across the spectrum of banking and financial services, so creating better capitalised entities capable of offering a wider spread of products and services and of competing head-on with international competitors in an increasingly demanding environment.

Another area now evolving further is Islamic banking and finance, and especially so in Bahrain. Whilst it is true to say this sector has moved forward increasingly fast between 1998 and 2002, especially when compared with the activity in the sector over the previous 20 years, the evidence suggests excellent potential continues to exist for the sector in years to come as more and more Muslims seek to perform their financial transactions in compliance with the Islamic *Shari'a.* The present activities of entities such as AAOIFI and the Liquidity Management Centre (LMC), allied to the efforts of the BMA, which is seeking to introduce new Islamically acceptable products, will all help in advancing the level of confidence in the sector in years to come and so ensure a greater public participation.

Integral to any growth in financial services in the coming years will be the enhanced use of information technology. Today, a number of banks within the GCC are able to offer their clients access to their accounts through automated teller machines (ATMs), over the telephone and, in some instances, over the Internet. Such clients may also be able to pay their staff electronically through direct fund transfer or pay their bills through ATMs, point-of-sale terminals (POS) or by debit and credit cards. Progress in this regard has beyond doubt been made, but over time, as more and more clients travel the world for business or pleasure, so they will want to conduct their business from afar and thus a major evolutionary step in the financial services sector is perceived likely to be the provision of enhanced services delivered electronically. Some banks in the region are well on their way to attaining this end but they, and many others which have yet to start, still have a long way to go.

In short, the evidence would suggest that the financial services industry in the future will see larger companies providing a wider array of financial products and services, both conventional and Islamic, frequently using information technology as the medium for their presentation and execution. The full implementation of the means to those ends is a major challenge for the financial sector, especially in the Middle East,

Yateem Mosque

and whilst far from insurmountable would seem likely to be a medium- to long-term activity with participants in Bahrain's international financial centre to the fore.

International cooperation and integration

For the global financial sector to succeed in the longer term there is strong evidence to suggest the need for increasing integration and cooperation both between national monetary and financial services authorities worldwide and with the companies that they oversee. As many financial institutions are now multi-national conglomerates, the future for many Gulf banks and financial companies lies in cross-border activities and closer coordination, to the extent of mergers and acquisitions, with their peers in neighbouring countries. As the pressure to attain and maintain global standards is likely to increase, so the need to enhance such activities is heightened.

For some time now the BMA has maintained very close relationships with financial authorities around the world, including those in London, New York, Hong Kong, Jersey, Malaysia and Singapore, whilst also proffering observations to committees of the GCC and other like bodies, to enable dialogue and overall enhancement of the level of understanding of international cross-border financial activities and, therefore, their effective regulation and supervision in line with global best practice. Such participation serves to ensure increased recognition of Bahrain as a well-regulated and supervised international financial centre whilst confirming its status as a leading global financial marketplace.

The need for international cooperation has been enhanced also by the need to seek to rein in criminal and terrorist activity by seeking to minimise money laundering and the financing of terrorism. In an increasingly global financial environment, where funds can flow rapidly from one jurisdiction to another at the press of a button, the need for an integrated approach towards stemming the flow goes unsaid. This is another major challenge for the financial community worldwide, and one which Bahrain pursues energetically.

It is the case also, that with financial institutions themselves operating in numerous locations and jurisdictions, there is an ongoing need for consistency in their regulation and supervision and thus close cooperation with the likes of the Basel Committee, the IMF and the Bank for International Settlements (BIS) becomes increasingly relevant.

Such cooperation and integration has grown markedly in recent years, with the BMA ensuring full participation along the way. But for the financial sector to survive with its reputation intact, operating with the full confidence of the consumer, the need for an integrated regulatory environment and ongoing cooperation globally is undoubted.

The future of the financial services sector

The financial services sector in Bahrain has come a long way since the mid-1970s and has become today much respected by international banks and financial institutions, regulatory authorities and by bodies such as the IMF. But the Government of Bahrain and the BMA are very ambitious, wishing to ensure the Kingdom remains at the forefront of international banking and finance for many years to come. To this end the BMA is working on developing a clear strategy for the future. In so doing great care is being taken to ensure maintenance of the country's reputation as a well-regulated, safe haven for the conduct of banking and finance.

In just over 25 years Bahrain has attained and maintained the status of number one financial location in the Middle East and has every intention of building on this not only by ensuring tangible development of the present activities of the institutions operating in the country but also by seeking to diversify the products and services being offered.

Already substantial attention has been given to developing Islamic banking and finance and, whilst much still needs to be done, the Kingdom is now host to the largest number of Islamic institutions of any financial centre in the Middle East. As the International Islamic Financial Market (IIFM) and the LMC grow in both size and volume of transactions and, over time, as new Islamic products and services are introduced, so it is anticipated Bahrain will become an even more important focal point for Islamic bankers and their customers.

In the conventional banking sector much thought has been given in recent times to the possibility of focusing attention on new asset classes, especially those areas where more business can be booked in Bahrain. Some high priority activities include financial trusts, with the country becoming an international location for their formation and management; the development of the debt and equity markets, including project finance, with services being offered by resident teams offering local knowledge, experience and expertise; and corporate and private banking, areas much in demand but frequently offered today from outside the region.

Now that Bahrain has a single regulator, other areas may also be opened up by the BMA. The potential exists for Bahrain to further increase its status as the regional insurance and reinsurance centre, a role it has played in the past through permitting the setting-up of so-called exempt (offshore) companies in the insurance sector, operating especially into Saudi Arabia. Integral to such thinking is the possibility of the country becoming a regional centre for captive insurance, specifically for major regional businesses. The Bahrain Stock Exchange (BSE) is also expected to develop further as part of the wider development of the equity market, with the ultimate aim of its becoming the leading stock market in the region cross-linked with other exchanges across the Middle East.

After detailed consideration, the BMA has, in mid-2003, endorsed a move to allow outsourcing services such as back-office functions, accounting and finance, information technology and human resources to be provided from Bahrain to banks and financial institutions. It is anticipated this addition to the services being offered locally will provide added value to the country's banking and financial industry and will become an area of substantial growth in the years to come.

Integral to these aims will be the provision of high-level services in what is a very competitive environment. To ensure the quality of the products and services being offered, the BMA is taking on a much wider role in providing technical assistance and comprehensive oversight whilst the Bahrain Institute for Banking and Finance (BIBF) continues to ensure training is provided so to provide professionally qualified staff to handle these increasingly sophisticated activities. The environment will continue to be competitive, of that there is no doubt. However, as new developments continue to be encouraged, the quality of the products and services being offered must be sustained and the inate professionalism of the people involved must be enhanced further still, so that Bahrain will grow and maintain its status as the financial capital of the Middle East well into the future.

Appendices

Appendix 1: Chronology of the history and development of Bahrain as a global financial market

1917	Establishment of the first money-changing business.
1921	Branch of Eastern Bank (now Standard Chartered Bank) is established.
1932	Oil is discovered.
1945	The Imperial Bank of Iran (now HSBC Middle East) opens a branch.
1950	First insurance agency, Norwich Union Fire Insurance Society, established.
1954	First Bahraini-owned insurance company, known as the Cooperative Compensation Society, formed.
1957	Bank of Bahrain (now National Bank of Bahrain) opens.
1958	Introduction of the Gulf rupee (to replace the Indian rupee).
1960	Arab Bank of Jordan opens a branch.
1964	Bahrain Currency Board established under Decree No. 6 (Finance).
1965	Bahraini dinar replaces the Gulf rupee, being introduced also in Abu Dhabi.
1970	Foundation stone laid for Aluminium Bahrain (Alba).
1971	Bahrain attains independence and joins the United Nations.
1972	Bahrain becomes a member of the International Monetary Fund and the International Bank for Reconstruction and Development.
1973	Bahrain Monetary Agency (BMA) established as successor to Bahrain Currency Board under Decree No. 23.
	Bahrain joins the Organisation of Arab Petroleum Exporting Countries (OAPEC).
	The Bahrain Government purchases 25 per cent of Bank of Bahrain, which becomes National Bank of Bahrain.
1974	Bahrain becomes a member of the Arab Fund for Economic and Social Development, the Arab Bank for Development in Africa and the Islamic Development Bank.

1975	The BMA issues its first licence for an Offshore Banking Unit (OBU) and for a money broker.
	First OBUs open - Citibank and Algemene Bank Nederland.
	Gulf International Bank, owned indirectly by the GCC States, commences operations.
	The establishment of offshore insurance companies is authorised by Ministerial Order.
	The first international money broker establishes a presence.
1976	Bahrain becomes a founder member of the Arab Monetary Fund.
1977	The first Investment Banking licence is issued to Bahrain Investment Bank.
	Licences for Representative Offices introduced.
	The first Government of Bahrain development bond issued.
	A Bahraini dinar Eurobond market is permitted to open.
	The first Bahraini dinar Eurobond is issued.
	Arab Shipbuilding and Repair Yard (ASRY) established sponsored by OAPEC.
1978	The Bahraini dinar is formally linked to Special Drawing Rights (SDR).
	The country's first Islamic bank is registered, Bahrain Islamic Bank.
1979	The Housing Bank is licensed and established.
	The Bankers' Society of Bahrain is established.
	Bahrain Islamic Bank commences operations.
	First offshore insurance company, Saudi International Insurance Co, is registered.
1980	Arab Banking Corporation, which was to become one of the largest banks by total assets in the Middle East, first registered.
	Arab Insurance Group (ARIG) established in Bahrain by the investment authorities of Abu Dhabi and Kuwait and the Government of Libya.
1981	The Bahrain Bankers' Training Centre (now Bahrain Institute of Banking and Finance) is established.
	The title of the chief executive of the BMA is changed from Director General to Governor.
	Bahrain becomes a member of the Gulf Cooperation Council (GCC).
	Bahrain Government becomes the majority shareholder in Bahrain Petroleum Co. (BAPCO).
1984	Money changers become subjected to BMA regulation for the first time.
1985	A money broker's code of conduct agreed between the banks, the BMA and the brokers.
	Gulf Petrochemical Industries Company (GPIC) comes on stream.
1986	The BMA holds the first auction of Bahrain Government Treasury bills.
1989	Bahrain Stock Exchange (BSE) opens.
	Takaful International, Bahrain's first Islamic insurance company, registered.
	Opening of new premises for the Bahrain Institute of Banking and Finance (formerly the Bankers' Training Centre).
1990	Insurance sector regulations introduced.
	Accounting and Auditing Organization for Islamic Financial Institutions (AAOIFI) formed.
1991	Bahrain Development Bank licensed and established.
	Locally incorporated banks and financial institutions are directed to comply with International Accounting Standards (IAS) by end 1992.

1992	Collective investment schemes, including mutual funds, subjected to new regulations introduced by the BMA.
	International Accounting Standards enforced for all banks and financial institutions by year end.
1993	BMA initiates the licensing, regulation and supervision of providers of investment and other financial services.
	Bahrain Insurance Association formed.
	Bahrain became a member of the General Agreement on Tariffs and Trade (GATT).
1994	Depositor Protection Scheme introduced by the BMA.
	Issuance of first licence for Investment Advisers and other Financial Services.
	Automated cheque clearing introduced.
	First corporate bonds quoted on the BSE.
	Insurance sector commitments made in preparation for membership of the World Trade Organisation (WTO).
1995	Bahrain becomes a member of the WTO.
	First mutual funds quoted on the BSE.
1996	Money changers become subjected to enhanced regulation by the BMA.
1997	Penalty system for dishonoured cheques introduced.
	Bahrain Government assumes full control of BAPCO and the Bahrain Refinery.
	Bahrain participated in the financial services negotiations of the WTO, submitting a schedule of banking sector and Stock Exchange commitments.
1998	New insurance broker regulations introduced to enhance the professionalism of the sector.
	ARIG Reinsurance Co. registered.
2000	Formation of the Islamic Financial Services Board agreed.
2001	The first Government of Bahrain Islamic leasing security (Sukuk al-ijarah) issued.
	The Bahraini dinar breaks its formal link with the SDR in favour of the US dollar as a first step to unification of the currencies of the GCC States by 2010 (possibly 2007).
	Prudential Regulations for Islamic Banks introduced.
	The first Sukuk al-salam (an Islamic form of Treasury bill) by a central bank is issued by the BMA.
	Government of Bahrain issues a Civil Code for the first time.
	General Council of Islamic Banks founded.
	Specific Council for Vocational Training (Banking Sector) formed.
2002	Bahrain becomes a Kingdom under Shaikh Hamad bin Isa Al Khalifa.
	BMA becomes the single regulatory body for the banking and financial sector, including insurance and the BSE.
	Liquidity Management Centre (LMC) set up.
	International Islamic Financial Market (IIFM) commences operations.
	International Islamic Rating Agency (IIRA) established.
	Regulations under study for trusts and insurance companies.
	Municipal and parliamentary elections held.

2003	BMA becomes a member of the International Association of Insurance Supervisors (IAIS). Human Resource Development Fund developed and introduced by the BMA with support from the Government. Centre for Research in Islamic Banking and Finance under creation. Bahrain's financial services commitments to the WTO updated. Bahrain's global financial market comprises 347 banks and financial institutions (180), insurance and insurance-related companies (154) and capital market brokers (13). Forty companies, of which five are registered outside Bahrain, are quoted on the BSE. LMC commences commercial operations. BMA issues first bond issue through an intermediary (the LMC). Insurance captives under study. Regulations for leasing companies issued. BMA's 950th issue of Treasury bills made.

Appendix 2: Offshore banking units as at 29 May 2003

- Ahli United Bank BSC
- AlBaraka Banking Group BSC (c)
- Allied Banking Corporation
- ALUBAF Arab International Bank EC
- Arab Asian Bank EC
- Arab Bank plc
- Arab Banking Corporation BSC
- Arab Investment Company SAA (The)
- Askari Commercial Bank
- Australia & New Zealand Banking Group Limited (ANZ)
- Bahrain International Bank EC
- Bahrain Middle East Bank EC
- BankMuscat SAOG
- Bank of Tokyo-Mitsubishi Ltd (The)
- Bank Saderat Iran
- BNP Paribas
- Citibank NA
- Citicorp Banking Corporation of Delaware
- Credit Agricole Indosuez
- Denizbank
- Disbank
- Finansbank AS
- Gulf Bank BSC
- Gulf International Bank BSC
- Gulf Investment Corporation
- Habib Bank Ltd
- Hong Kong & Shanghai Banking Corporation Limited (The)
- HSBC Bank AS
- HSBC Bank Middle East
- International Banking Corporation (The)
- JP Morgan Chase Bank
- Kocbank AS
- Korea Exchange Bank
- Kuwait Turkish Evkaf Finance House
- Malayan Banking Berhad (Maybank)
- Mashreq Bank psc
- Muslim Commercial Bank Ltd.
- National Bank of Abu Dhabi
- National Bank of Kuwait SAK
- National Bank of Pakistan
- Oyak Bank AS
- Pamukbank TAS
- Saudi National Commercial Bank (The)
- Shamil Bank of Bahrain EC (Islamic Bankers)
- Standard Chartered Bank plc
- State Bank of India
- Turk Ekonomi Bankasi
- Turkiye Garanti Bankasi AS
- Turkiye Is Bankasi AS
- Woori Bank
- Yapi ve Kredi Bankasi AS

Appendix 3: Investment banks as at 29 May 2003

ABC Islamic Bank EC	First Islamic Investment Bank EC
ABC Islamic Fund EC	Gulf Finance House BSC EC
Al-Amin Bank BSC EC	International Credit Company BSC (c)
AlBaraka Islamic Bank BSC EC	International Investment Bank BSC EC
AlKhaleej Islamic Investment Bank BSC EC	Investcorp Bank EC
Amex (Middle East) EC	Investors Bank EC
Arab Financial Services Company EC	Khaleej Finance and Investment
Arab Islamic Bank EC	Liquidity Management Centre BSC (c)
Bahrain Financing Co.	Man Ahli Investment Bank EC
Bahrain Investment Bank BSC	Merrill Lynch International Bank Limited
Capital Investment Holding Co. EC	Nomura Investment Banking (Middle East) EC
Capital Union EC (c)	Noriba Bank BSC (c)
Card Company EC (The)	Overland Leasing Bank BSC (c)
Citi Islamic Investment Bank EC	Securities & Investment Company BCSC
Credimax	Societe General Asset Management (SGAM) Bahrain EC
Daiwa Securities SMBC Europe Limited, Middle East Branch	TAIB Bank EC
Diners Club Services Bahrain WLL	UBS Global Asset Management
Faysal Investment Bank of Bahrain EC	United Gulf Bank BSC EC

Appendix 4: Representative offices as at 29 May 2003

Aberdeen Asset Managers	International Investment Group
Alliance Capital Limited	Lend Lease Investment limited
American Express Bank Ltd.	Man Investment Products Limited
American Express International Inc.	Mellon Global Investment Markets Ltd.
Bank of Bermuda (The)	Merrill Lynch Bank (Suisse) SA
BNP Paribas	Merrill Lynch Investment Managers Limited
Citicorp Investment Bank	MFS International Limited
Commerzbank AG	Mizuho Corporate bank Ltd
Credit Agricole Indosuez	Murray Johnstone Limited
Deutsche Bank AG	Robeco Institutional Asset Management BV
First Union National Bank	Robeco USA LLC
GNI Fund Management (Gerrard & National Inter Commodities)	Robert Fleming Holdings Limited
HSBC Bank plc	Sumitomo Mitsui Banking Corporation
International Commercial Bank of China (The)	UBS AG
	Wasserstein Middle East

Appendix 5: Companies listed on the Bahrain Stock Exchange 31 May 2003

BAHRAINI COMPANIES

Commercial bank sector

National Bank of Bahrain
Bank of Bahrain & Kuwait
Ahli United Bank
Bahrain Islamic Bank
The Bahraini Saudi Bank

Investment sector

Gulf Monetary Group
Arab Banking Corporation
United Gulf Bank
Bahrain International Bank
Investcorp Bank
Bahrain Middle East Bank
Bahrain Commercial Facilities Co.
United Gulf Industries Co.
TAIB Bank
Shamil Bank of Bahrain

Insurance sector

Bahrain Kuwait Insurance Co.
Al-Ahlia Insurance Co.
Arab International Insurance Co.
Takaful International Co.
Arab Insurance Group
Bahrain National Holding Co.

Service sector

Bahrain Ship Repairing & Engineering Co.
Bahrain Cinema Co.
National Import & Export Co.
General Trading & Food Processing Co.
Bahrain Maritime & Mercantile International
Bahrain Telecommunications Co.
Bahrain Car Park Co.
Bahrain Duty Free Shop Complex Co.

Industrial sector

Bahrain Flour Mills Co.
Delmon Poultry Co.

Hotel & tourism sector

Bahrain Hotels Co.
National Hotels Co.
Bahrain Tourism Co.
Bahrain Family Leisure Co.

Closed company sector

Securities and Investment Company

NON-BAHRAINI COMPANIES

International Investment Group (Kuwait)
The International Investors (Kuwait)
Sudan Telecommunications Company (Sudan)
Qatar Telecommunications Company (Qatar)
BankMuscat (Oman)

Bibliography

Activities of the Insurance Market in Bahrain 2000 and 2001, Bahrain Monetary Agency.

Annual Insurance Report 2002, Ministry of Commerce and Industry.

Annual Report 2000, Bahrain Institute of Banking and Finance.

Annual Report 2000, Bahrain Monetary Agency.

Annual Report 2000, Bahrain Stock Exchange.

Bahrain: A Heritage Explored, Angela Clarke, MEED Books, 1986.

Bahrain – An International Banking and Financial Centre, The Bankers' Society of Bahrain.

Bahrain – An International Financial Centre, 1994, Bahrain Monetary Agency.

Bahrain Development Bank, *Annual Report* 2000 and 2001.

Bahrain Development Bank, *Financing Business Enterprise.*

Bahrain Development Bank, *Programmes and Guidelines.*

Bahrain Dinar Digest, Issue 1, Volume 1, January 2002, Bahrain Monetary Agency.

Bahrain Dinar Digest, Issue 1, Volume 2, July 2002, Bahrain Monetary Agency.

Bahrain Dinar Digest, Issue 2, Volume 1, January 2003, Bahrain Monetary Agency.

Bahrain Fact File, *World Link*, October 2000.

Bahrain Insurance Association – Constitution.

Bahrain Monetary Agency Law, Decree, Law No (23) of 1973.

Bahrain Stock Exchange, A Presentation, Hani Al-Mandeel, 2001.

Bahrain Stock Exchange, *Annual Reports.*

Bahrain Stock Exchange, *Fact Books*, 1999 and 2000.

Bahrain Stock Exchange Information Folder, 1999 and 2000.

Bahrain Stock Exchange Law, Decree, Law 4/1987.

Bahrain Stock Exchange, *The Right Choice for Listing in the Region*, Bahrain Stock Exchange – 2001.

Bankers' Society of Bahrain – Constitution.

Building a New Insurance Regulatory Framework, Consultation Paper 1: Insurance Captives, April 2003, Bahrain Monetary Agency.

Centre Brief, 1999 and 2000 Annual Reports, Press Releases and Circulars.

Corporate Structure of the Bahrain Monetary Agency.

Currency Issues of the State of Bahrain, Ahmed Qarata.

Currency Museum Folder, Bahrain Monetary Agency.

Doing Business in Bahrain, Ernst & Young.

Doing Business with Bahrain, February 2002, Kogan Page.

Financial Institution and Islamic Bank details.

Financial trust Regulation in the Kingdom of Bahrain, Trowers & Hamlins, 2002.

Helping to build a better Bahrain, The Housing Bank.

History of Currency in the State of Bahrain, The Bahrain Monetary Agency, 1996.

Institutions in Bahrain, Parts 1 – 3.

Insurance Legislation, Amiri Decrees 3 and 17, 1987 and *Implementing Regulation* No.6 1990, Ministry of Commerce and Agriculture, Directorate of Commerce and Company Affairs.

International Financial Statistics Yearbook, 1994, International Monetary Fund.

International Financial Statistics, April 2002, International Monetary Fund.

Investors Guide, Bahrain, Economic Development Board.

Investors Guide to Bahrain, United Nations Industrial Development Organisation.

Islamic Banking and Finance in the Kingdom of Bahrain, Bahrain Monetary Agency, Editor: Brian Kettell.

'Islamic Banking Hub Bahrain', *Quarterly Newsletter*, Issue 1, April 2003, Bahrain Monetary Agency.

Licensed Banks and Financial Institutions in Bahrain, Licensing & Information Unit, Bahrain Monetary Agency, 31st March 2002.

Materials on the BMA Web Site including Historical Background, International Anti-Money Laundering Regulation.

National Accounts 2001, Economic Affairs, Directorate of Economic Planning, Ministry of Finance and National Economy.

National Bank of Bahrain Information Brochure.

Norwich Union, The First 200 Years.

Objectives and Functions, Bahrain Stock Exchange.

Preparing for the Future, Exploring the Market Potential and Opportunities for Foreign Investment, Bahrain Stock Exchange, 2000.

Prudential Information & Regulatory Framework for Islamic Banks, The Bahrain Monetary Agency.

Quarterly Statistical Bulletin, September 1977, Bahrain Monetary Agency.

Quarterly Statistical Bulletin, December 1986, Bahrain Monetary Agency.

Quarterly Statistical Bulletin, September 1995, Bahrain Monetary Agency.

Quarterly Statistical Bulletin, December 1995, Bahrain Monetary Agency.

Quarterly Statistical Bulletin, December 1998, Bahrain Monetary Agency.

Quarterly Statistical Bulletin, December 2001, Bahrain Monetary Agency.

Quarterly Statistical Bulletin, March 2002, Bahrain Monetary Agency.

Quarterly Statistical Bulletin, December 2002, Bahrain Monetary Agency.

Regulation of Islamic Banks, Anwar Khalifa Al-Sadah.

Regulations Governing Collective Investment Schemes and Financial Trusts.

Standard Conditions and Licensing Criteria, Bahrain Monetary Agency.

The BIA News, Bahrain Insurance Association, 2001.

The BMA as an Integrated Regulator, Dr. Khalid Ateeq and Ralph Ricks, 2002.

The Deposit Protection Scheme of Bahrain, Bahrain Monetary Agency.

The Establishment, Regulation and Supervision of Banks and Other Financial Institutions in Bahrain, Part 1 – Licensing; Part 2 – Regulation; Part 3 – Circulars.

The Law, Bahrain Stock Exchange.